"Every so often a book comes along that ingeniously does our home-work for us. Rev. Seifert and Dr. Urbine's digest of magisterial teaching on marriage and the family illustrates the resiliency of the church in finding fresh ways to give us a vision of Catholic teaching on the fami-ly. Anyone looking for a confident and positive compass about family values today will find it in this book.

"Teachers will love its instant syllabus. Those involved in marriage preparation will find a superb overview. My own copy will be well thumbed in the years to come."

Rev. Alfred McBride, O.Praem.
Pope John XXIII National Seminary

"*On Life and Love* is an excellent resource. The authors capture the es-sence of each document in clear and concise language, while placing each document in its historical context. The format, study questions, and resources are very helpful. I wish such a resource existed for other church documents! An admirable job!"

Theresa Notare
U.S.C.C., National Family Planning

"*On Life and Love* will be a valuable tool for the student as well as the pastoral minister. In a well-organized and succinct manner it makes available the most representative documents of modern church teach-ing on marriage and family life. This compendium makes it possible to see what the church has consistently taught and to appreciate how our teaching on marriage and family life has undergone necessary develop-ment over the years. The section on 'key themes' is especially useful for one who wants to locate an idea in one or more of the documents and then study it in context."

H. Richard McCord, Associate Director
N.C.C.B. Committee on Marriage and Family

"Where was this resource when I was preparing for family ministry? Yet even now this book is a great help to me because it provides me with a single source to locate numerous references that will assist me in presentations, workshops, and writings. It demonstrates the im-portance and prominence of family life and will no doubt aid in the de-velopment of a greater consciousness about the value and dignity of the Christian family today. I heartily recommend it."

Don Paglia
President, National Association
of Diocesan Family Life Directors

William Urbine & William Seifert

On *Life* and *Love*

A Guide to Catholic Teaching on Marriage and Family

TWENTY-THIRD PUBLICATIONS

Mystic, Connecticut 06355

Acknowledgments

We wish to recognize the kind permission of Orbis Books to adapt and modify the format used in Peter Henriot, Edward P. DeBerri, Michael J. Schultheis's *Catholic Social Teaching: Our Best Kept Secret* (Centenary Edition), Maryknoll, NY: Orbis Books, © 1992 (3rd rev. ed.).

We are grateful to Our Sunday Visitor Press for the use of the outline in their pamphlet on *The Vatican Declaration on Certain Questions Regarding Sexual Ethics.*

We also wish to note the incalculable debt to the scholarship and work of Sr. Claudia Carlen, I.H.M. for her compendium *The Papal Encyclicals* (vols. 1-5), Raleigh, NC: The Pieran Press, © 1990, and its related work *Papal Pronouncements* (vols. 1-2), Raleigh, NC: The Pieran Press, © 1990. The bulk of the key quotations are taken from these volumes.

Twenty-Third Publications
185 Willow Street
P.O. Box 180
Mystic CT 06355
(203) 536-2611
800-321-0411

ISBN 0-89622-570-4
Library of Congress Catalog Card Number 93-60402
Printed in the U.S.A.

Foreword

On Life and Love: A Guide to Catholic Teaching on Marriage and Family Life is a very useful compilation of church documents in outline form. It is especially timely in light of the contemporary and widespread assumptions that the family as we know it is passé and will shortly be replaced by new family forms. We are continually told of the rising rates of divorce, out-of-wedlock pregnancy, family violence, abortions, and increasing numbers of people simply cohabiting. Scholars of the family have recently noted that these phenomena challenge family life and that the overemphasis on individualism, sexual libertarianism, and rejection of social traditions regarding the family are destructive both for individual persons and for society. In the face of all this, social institutions—including the churches—have grown silent and have failed to support and reinforce the basic aspirations of people. But the scholars also tell us that the vast majority of Americans hope for a faithful and personally enriching partnership, a stable family, sufficient security—financial and otherwise—to bring children into the world and raise them with hope and vision.

This is where *On Life and Love* can be especially helpful. The book presents the fundamental points of the church's teaching as it has unfolded and developed since apostolic times. It focuses especially on the articulation of that teaching by modern popes and the Second Vatican Council. It gives a comprehensive and integral view of the teaching and applies it to contemporary issues and challenges. A work of this kind will be most useful to those doing research in the area of marriage and family life.

The church's teaching is based on respect for each person who is created by God and redeemed by Jesus Christ. Our human dignity rests on God's creative love and on our capacity for spiritual growth and eternal union with God. As the Second Vatican Council has reminded us, "The well-being of the individual person and of human and Christian society is intimately linked with the healthy condition of that community produced by marriage and the family" (Church in the Modern World, 47).

The Christian family, then, is not simply a social institution, but part of God's overall plan of redemption. It is a communion of persons who inspire, enrich, reconcile one another and accompany one another on their spiritual journeys. As Pope John Paul II tells us, Christian marriage and the Christian family build up the church and enable it to carry on Christ's mission in our world. The Christian family is at the service of life; it takes an active role in developing a society that respects human dignity and human rights and it continues to proclaim Christ's message of love and unity.

It is both pastorally necessary and enriching to affirm the church's teaching on human sexuality, the sanctity of life, the sacredness of marriage and family life to young people, especially those preparing for marriage. *On Life and Love* will enable pastoral ministers, teachers, and counselors to draw on the church's wisdom and pastoral insights and to help people see marriage and family life as vocation, sacrament, and covenant.

Most Reverend James T. McHugh
Bishop of Camden

Contents

Dedication

To our families who have nurtured us

My wife Christine
and children: Andrew, Timothy, Alicia, Katie

Our Parents
Walter and Lucy Seifert
Anthony and Frances Urbine

Introduction

Students and small children, spouses and pastors keep us honest. All of them have asked us, "Why would anyone want to put out a book on church documents?" It's a very good question. There has to be some reason for writing a book about the statements that popes, national conferences of bishops, and papal commissions make public. Both of us are teachers with much classroom, scholarly, and pastoral experience. There have been many times when it would have been helpful to have some source that would bring large pronouncements into a human view. Our hope is to make the Church's teaching and wisdom about marriage and family life more understandable. This is what we have proposed to do in this book. Some guiding questions clarify our purpose :

• Why study the contemporary teaching of the Roman Catholic Church on marriage and family issues?

• What statements about marriage and family life have been published and why do they matter? Who are they written for?

• Are the Church documents relevant and worth reading?

• Why aren't these documents better read?

• How are we going to examine these documents?

• How can this book be used?

Why study the contemporary teaching of the Roman Catholic Church on marriage and family issues?
In the middle of the nineteenth century, the Catholic Church sought to respond to the crisis of faith brought about by the philosophical systems arising from the post-reformation era, and particularly those of the enlightenment. The emphasis on the empirical sciences led to a de-

nial of God and organized religion and to the rise of a purely secular vision of human destiny. The resulting rejection of any religious vision led to a denial of the authority of the Church in the area of marriage and family life. The Church's response led to Vatican Council I and subsequent official statements.

Over the last one hundred years the Roman Catholic Church has presented numerous statements on marriage and family issues to the world. They are meant to guide and direct the people of God in their pilgrimage of faith. The Church is concerned that the values of marriage and family life, seen within a sacramental context, be understood and accepted as achievable goals for individuals, couples, and families to live within their lives. Many of these documents were developed as a result of direct questions posed to church leadership. These formal statements have often been misunderstood and even distorted because of the publicity surrounding their announcement. Some provide a broad theological view while others focus on specific areas of the Christian life.

This book will summarize key documents on marriage and family life over the last century in a way that is concise and understandable. The historical setting, crucial to understanding the need for the statement, will also be given.

What statements about marriage and family life have been published and why do they matter? Who are they written for?
There is no simple answer to these complex questions. A distinction between the kinds of statements the Church makes and their particular authoritative weight is vital. Several written statements have gone through a complicated process of formation. Sometimes spoken statements are made by Church officials and are put "on the record" later, but not all statements have the same importance; not every Church leader has the same authority.

In the past century the popes have made many strong and supportive statements on marriage and family issues. This study of Church statements includes all the *official* Church teachings and so does not focus exclusively upon papal statements.

It is important for the laity, vowed religious, and clergy alike to recognize and acknowledge the authoritative nature of the Church's teaching. Each of the statements presented here was prepared with considerable consultation, much discussion, and abundant prayer. These teachings are understood to be the "ordinary teaching" of the Roman Catholic Church. None of the statements presented has yet been defined as *infallible*. We believe that the Holy Spirit, given to the Church in its origin by Christ himself, guides the Church in its teaching mission, and preserves it as it responds to the command of Jesus to "...teach all nations." These "ordinary" teachings are those that have withstood the scrutiny of time and have been accepted and taught by the Church throughout the ages. Each of these documents reflects the particular guidance of the Holy Spirit and the cumulative wisdom of the universal Church throughout history. Each statement participates in the mission of Christ and should be reflected upon with a sense of respect that acknowledges its authoritative nature.

Many of these statements are directed toward "target audiences" of scholars and theologians and can be difficult to understand. There can be a real and frustrating conflict between a statement that is directed to theologians and a teaching that enlivens one's faith. Good will only goes so far in assisting one's analyses here. There is need for more. The task of this work, then, is to assist the good will of those who would understand the Church's profound truths by examining the documents at hand.

Are the Church documents relevant and worth reading?

The word relevance has been trivialized by overuse, yet here it is a vital concept. These statements are worth reading because they reflect the teaching of the Church, which is the guidance of the Holy Spirit given to us on a variety of issues. Many of the critical concerns raised across the past century have not changed, nor have their responses. In each generation the people of God hear the consistent message through new voices.

Why aren't these documents more widely read?

Frankly, they are tough to read, hardly exciting, and even boring. The manner of presentation and the choice of words reflect styles that may seem out of date to many. Often these statements seem very dry and abstract. Because they deal with significant issues, they obviously are not light reading. Written with a universal (catholic in the clearest sense) vision, they often appear out of touch with a modern perspective or too general to be useful. In fact, they are not. One common retort to Church statements is that "...actions speak louder than words" and that the Church should go beyond saying what should be done to actually doing what Jesus wants. There is merit to this admonition, still the Church continually calls itself to action and challenges the Body of Christ to make the Gospel of Christ thrive in each generation.

One tool for this challenge are statements that vigorously reaffirm the virtues of marriage and family life in a changing world. The statements of the teaching Church affirm the dedicated activity of individual Christians who, throughout their daily pursuits, strive to uphold the Gospel of salvation in their lives. Individuals and families need to appreciate that the values they hold so dear are the ones that the Church proclaims and treasures as part of the Teaching of Christ.

How are we going to examine these documents?

The cultural perspective of a North American Catholic differs from that of other Christians throughout the world. The issues for Roman Catholics in Brazil differ from those of Canada. It is necessary to examine the levels of church teaching on marriage and family that have been presented over the past 100 years. A survey of the cultural and historical background is crucial to avoid misunderstandings.

As this work is an introduction to the Church's teaching, it is also an invitation to the reader to move beyond the clear limits of this book and read the richness of these teachings in their full translations. The bibliography and the suggestions for further reading will provide resources where the reader will be able to consult with original sources as well as authoritative translations of the documents reviewed here.

Our method is simple. Each statement will be examined in its historical context, then thematically reviewed. The development of the statement provides a richer and necessary appreciation for the placement of the statement in the body of Church teachings. An outline and summary of points will follow. Specific sections and their significance to the interested reader will be highlighted, and points of linkage to the social justice teaching of the Church will be included. A list of suggested readings and a pertinent quotation will be found at the end of each document's summary. Section (§) and paragraph (¶) symbols indicate the pertinent references within the specific document at hand.

How can this book be used?

Why did *we* write this book? We began this section with that question and hope these final points bring things into focus. Over the years both of us have had to outline and present summaries of these documents for classroom use. Our expertise overlaps in the areas of family therapy and family education. Early in our association we began to exchange insights and ideas. We also began to share methods and materials. In time, our presentations got easier and clearer and our theological vision, tempered in pastoral experience and academic work, was broadened and deepened. It seemed sensible to share what we've done with our colleagues.

This book provides an overview of critical documents touching upon marriage and family issues over the past hundred years. Students will find it possible to uncover specific themes that emerge among the written pronouncements of the Church in this area. This provides a more critical awareness of the integrity of the Church's tradition and the dynamism of its reasoning as it meets the critical issues of the day. Readers will find access to the primary documents much easier and more desirable.

Teachers will find the volume useful for these same reasons. Additionally, they will be able to direct the students to particular documents and themes more easily. The outline format provides a lucid ground to make general presentations and for comparing documents with one another. The study questions help both the teacher and the students to look beyond the details of a particular document to the broader issues that have been addressed over the last century. We hope they are great test questions too.

College and graduate educators can find this book useful along with specific primary sources in courses on marriage and family life. The brief history and bibliography are a springboard to deeper reflection and resources.

Those in pastoral ministry are often called upon to make "quick" presentations on substantive topics. We are aware of the real limits pastoral care workers experience. This work provides an easy set of outlines on key themes and topics in this area. Also, people often ask for specific answers to questions that no one has the time to research in depth. This book is a good starting point to help others to probe the wealth of the Church's teaching.

Overview: Christian Marriage

The Tradition of the Roman Catholic Church through the 20th Century

Pope Leo XIII to Vatican II
Responding to the Social and Moral Needs of a New World

The Church's modern expression of its teaching on marriage and family life is first encountered in Pope Leo XIII's encyclical letter *Arcanum* (*On Christian Marriage*). Although not fully appreciated by many today, the direction begun by Leo XIII is ground breaking. This document was written eleven years prior to *Rerum Novarum* (*The Condition of Labor*). It marks the beginning of the Church's contemporary effort to address the social conditions and concerns of married couples and their families. The placement of family life and the relationship between husband and wife at the heart of social teaching emerges as a decisive contribution of Roman Catholic teaching.

In reaffirming the scholastic understanding of the purposes of marriage, Leo XIII addresses the critical issues of the day: state interference in family matters, civil divorce, and the assault within society upon the stability of marriage. Through this teaching, Leo solidly upholds the sacramentality of marriage as instituted by God from the beginning, and as a source of special graces for the spouses, enabling the generation of family life.

Begun under the direction of Leo XIII and completed during the pontificate of Benedict XV, the Roman Catholic Church created its first unified Code of Canon Law. Within this code, four chapters (cc. 1012-

1057) summarize the key juridical concerns about matrimony. They are: general provisions about marriage, the impediments to sacramental marriage, valid consent and the form of marriage, the dissolution of marriage, separation in marriage, and convalidation of a civil marriage. *Arcanum* strongly accentuates the contractual responsibilities of matrimony, and the two purposes of marriage (procreation of offspring and stability of the spousal union) are stated clearly. This approach is continued in the code. Canon 1013 of the 1917 code asserts:

> sec. 1 The primary end of marriage is the procreation and education of children; its secondary end is mutual help and the allaying of concupiscence.

> sec. 2 The essential properties of marriage are unity and indissolubility, which acquire a peculiar firmness in Christian marriage by reason of its sacramental character.

In 1930 [December 31—The Feast of the Holy Family], on the occasion of the 50th anniversary of *Arcanum*, Pope Pius XI issued the encyclical *Casti Connubii (On Christian Marriage)*. Given the worldwide economic situation at the time, and the rise of various socialist and Marxist theories and practices, *Casti Connubii* reaffirms the three goods of marriage stated by St. Augustine and reiterates the goods and obligations of parenthood as well as the indissolubility and stability of marriage. Like the prior document *Arcanum*, it addresses social concerns—for example, cohabitation and contraception.

During the period of the Second World War (1939-1945) little formal documentation was addressed to the area of marriage and family life. In the post-war era (1946-1956), Pope Pius XII addressed specific concerns to those professions that assisted families. Most notable are his addresses to midwives, physicians, medical specialists, and family associations. In *Vegliare Con Sollecitudine (Address to Midwives;* October 29, 1951) and *Nell'Ordine Della (Address to the Association of Larger Families;* November 26, 1951), Pius XII, building upon the foundation laid by Pius XI, sets forth key ideas that will emerge in subsequent papal teachings. He states: "Every human being, even a child in the mother's womb, has a right to life directly from God and not from the parents or from any human society or authority" (Liebard, 104, §272). He reaffirms the twofold ends of marriage, highlighting the critical role of procreation and education of children.

Pope John XXIII, Paul VI, and Vatican II

The updating of the Church, which began with the philosophical work under Leo XIII, led to an even more aggressive updating within the forum of a general council. John XXIII's unforeseen convocation of this general council reflected the hope for a renewal of the Church in the modern world.

John XXIII's supervision and influence within the council enabled it to move beyond a reified vision of church and society that had been proposed in the draft schemata prior to first session of the council. Along with the emphasis on the role of the laity emerging from the declarations of Vatican II, came a greater focus on the concerns of marriage and family life. The two "ends" of marriage—communion of life and of love—were reasserted within a personalistic framework. A pastoral vision of marriage and family was expressed in *Gaudium et Spes* (the *Pastoral Constitution on the Church in the Modern World*).

The 1969 revision of the *Rite of Marriage* made most clear that priority be given to the formation of the family even before the exchange of consent in the celebration of the rite. The revised rite specifically called for the deepened participation of the marrying couple in the development of society. A new appreciation for interfaith marriage was noted in this document and subsequent documents. Ecumenical collaboration developed as a result of the new emphasis on healing the divisions among the churches (cf. *The Decree on Ecumenism*, Anglican/Catholic and Baptist/Catholic Dialogues).

From Vatican II To Present

Paul VI and Humanae Vitae

Pope John XXIII called for a commission to address critical social issues of population growth, family planning, and birth regulation. This commission, established during the council, was comprised of specialists including medical, counseling, theological, and pastoral experts. The questions raised at this time led many observers to expect that the Church would depart from prior and consistent teaching on contraception. In an address to the Special Pontifical Commission Paul VI presented the problem in this manner:

> In what forms and according to what forms ought married couples, in exercising their love for each other, fulfill this life-giving function to which their vocation calls them? The Christian answer will always be inspired by an awareness of the duties of the married state, of its dignity—the love of the Christian spouses, being ennobled by the grace of the sacrament—

and of the grandeur of the gift bestowed upon the child who is called to life. (Liebard, *Love and Sexuality*, 269)

The commission did not reach any consensus, but rather issued two reports in 1966. This resulted in Paul VI's personal intervention, which reaffirmed the teaching of the Magisterium, employing the traditional grounds (natural law basis) against artificial contraception. While somewhat unexpected in theological circles, Paul VI's considerations are firmly grounded within the Tradition.

A number of national bishops' conferences, including those of the United States, England, Germany, Canada, and Australia wrote pastoral reflections supporting the teaching and its application among the faithful. The theological firestorm that followed caused considerable reflection upon many connected issues, most notably the authority of the Church to teach in matters of sexual ethics.

In an address to the Teams of Our Lady (May 4, 1970), Paul VI sets forth a pastoral application of the teaching found in the encyclical *Humanae Vitae*. He notes:

As holy scripture teaches us, marriage is a great earthly reality before it is a sacrament: "God created man to his own image; to the image of God he created him. Male and Female he created them." We must always return to this first chapter of the bible if we wish to know what a married couple, a family is and ought to be. Psychological analysis, psychoanalytic studies, sociological inquiries and philosophical reflections can certainly shed their own ray of light on sexuality and human love, but they would delude us if they neglected this basic lesson that was given to us at the very start. The duality of the sexes has been willed by God, so that man and woman together might be the image of God and like him, a source of life: "Be fruitful and multiply, fill the earth and subdue it." (Liebard, 379 §1341)

This foreshadows the insights of Pope John Paul II as he began his reflections upon the nature of marriage and family life.

Throughout the 1970s the Church was challenged by strong positions and opinions, especially on the topics of sexuality, gender roles, and divorce. The Church reaffirmed its teaching on specific aspects of sexual ethics in 1975 in a document issued by the Sacred Congregation for the Doctrine of the Faith.

Pope John Paul II (1978 - Present)
The death of Paul VI in 1978 was followed by the election of Albino Lu-

ciani, a member of the pontifical commission of John XXIII. His pontificate lasted less than a month. His sudden death led to the election of the first non-Italian pope in 500 years. With John Paul II's strong philosophical and theological understandings, expressed through phenomenological language, the presentation of the teachings of the Church took on a new direction.

The first synod of bishops called by John Paul II addressed marriage and family issues. It resulted in the publication of the Apostolic Exhortation *Familiaris Consortio* in 1981. (It also resulted in the establishment of a separate faculty for the explicit study of marriage and family issues under his personal patronage.) The document focuses upon four critical tasks of the family—the formation of a community of persons, serving new life, participating in the development of society, sharing in the life and mission of the Church. A fully developed theology of conjugal spirituality is also expressed. The document suggests pastoral strategies to assist families, in particular: mixed marriages, civil marriages, the separated and divorced and widowed.

Early in his pontificate, John Paul II used the Wednesday midday audiences to build an explicit theology of the body, using the Scriptures (Genesis, Ephesians, Gospels) within a personalistic structure. While not intended to be used as a magisterial teaching, these audiences both reflect the breadth and depth of insight of the pontiff and appear within subsequent exhortations and teachings.

Alongside these key initiatives of John Paul II are the specific responses by various Vatican offices during the 1970s and 1980s on current concerns—including reproductive technologies, the sexual orientation of the human person, the dignity and role of women, and the rights of families in society.

The Code of Canon Law, which was initiated as a result of Vatican II, was promulgated in 1983 and completes the theological vision of the council. With the personal examination and review of Pope John Paul II, the code shows a shift in focus. The section on Marriage (cc. 1055–1165) strongly affirms the covenantal basis for sacramental marriage while also maintaining the contractual element of marriage. Canon 1055 notes:

> 1055.1 The marriage covenant by which a man and a woman establish between themselves a partnership of their whole life, and which of its own very nature is ordered to the well being of the spouses and to the procreation and upbringing of children, has, between the baptized, been raised by Christ the Lord to the dignity of a sacrament.

> 1055.2 Consequently, a valid marriage contract cannot exist be-

tween baptized persons without it being by that very fact a sacrament.

In light of the revision of the Code of Canon Law and its influence upon pastoral and liturgical practice, the revised rite of marriage (1990) continues to promote the unity of the theological, pastoral, and sacramental life begun in matrimony. It presents a renewed emphasis on the local pastor and the community's responsibility to encourage the faith life and practice of the engaged couple.

In 1990 the Code of Canons for the Oriental Church was promulgated by the Holy See. The vision of the Second Vatican Council guided the formation of this revised code for the churches of the Eastern Rites. The importance of this code cannot be overlooked, as these canons reflect the rich spirituality of the oriental churches and guide the pastoral and liturgical practices of these rites.

In the years following Vatican Council II, the need for suitable catechetical materials expressive of the insights of the council and the modern church became apparent. The Roman Catechism of the Council of Trent provided the church with an instrument for Catholic education that served the church admirably. *The Catechism of the Catholic Church* provides the Church of Christ with a compendium of material from which the catechetical mandate of Christ will reach into the twenty-first century. The section on the sacraments and marriage are noteworthy. As of this writing, only French, Spanish, and Italian editions are available. A review of the catechism is not included in this book for that reason.

The United States Bishops Respond

In the United States, the Catholic bishops responded to marriage and family concerns through pastoral statements in the 1940s and 1950s. These statements responded to issues rooted in the transitions occurring in society at that time. In response to *Humanae Vitae*, the U.S. bishops' pastoral letter *Human Life in Our Day* (1969) supported Paul VI's teaching. In 1978 they issued *The Plan of Pastoral Action for Family Ministry: A Vision and Strategy*. It called for a process (of family ministry) directed to an awareness that understands, a caring that enables, a ministry that serves, and structures that truly facilitate.

In 1987 *A Family Perspective in Church and Society* was issued by the National Conference of Catholic Bishops (NCCB). The document challenged the church and society to view its policies, programs, ministries, and services from a family perspective. Advocating on behalf of the needs of families, the document *Putting Children and Families First* was issued in 1992. In 1994 a statement entitled *Follow the Way of Love*, highlighting the United Nations International Year of the Family, is being published by the American bishops.

One Hundred Years of Social Teaching
Affirming Marriage and Family

Clearly linked to the documentation on marriage and family is the hundred years of Roman Catholic social teaching. This teaching, from Leo XIII's *Rerum Novarum* to John Paul II's *Socialis Rei,* is rooted in the historical moment. This body of teachings addresses the pressing issues of the day, responding to the prevailing philosophy of the moment from the Catholic Tradition. It weaves themes of support for marriage and family within it—from the question of a just wage for those with families (*Rerum*) to recent statements about the role of women in the workplace (*Laborem Exercens*). A brief summary of key social documents as they relate to marriage and family teaching is found on pages 103-105.

Key Themes

I. The Divine Origins of Institution of Marriage

Marriage is far more than a secular reality. It has its origin within the very nature of human relationships. God is the author of the human person and as such instituted marriage as both a divine and human institution. (*Arcanum, Casti Connubii, Gaudium et Spes, Familiaris Consortio*)

II. The Sacred and the Ordinary

The writings of the contemporary teaching authority of the Church present a clear emphasis on the presence of God within ordinary events. Applied to marriage, this theme moves beyond former juridical definitions in a significant way to God within the daily experiences of marriage and family. (*Gaudium et Spes, Familiaris Consortio*)

III. The Dignity of the Human Person in Community

From conception to the time of death, human beings are communal or social beings. The primary and formative community is the family. Human dignity is uncovered and promoted first and foremost in the family. (*Arcanum, Familiaris Consortio, Humanae Vitae, Donum Vitae*)

IV. The Theology of the Body

The dignity of the human person is founded upon a unified reality. This bodily/spiritual reality exists from the moment of conception until death. One's identity is grounded within this unified experience. Human sexuality develops within and is integral to this unified nature. Gender is the vehicle through which human beings relate. (*Familiaris Consortio, Mulieris Dignitatem, Pastoral Care of the Homosexual, Persona Humana*)

V. The Dignity and Equality of Sexes

The fullness of being human incorporates our sexuality. Male and Female are two ways of experiencing humanity. Biblical theology strongly emphasizes the original dignity of each gender and their essential complementarity. Recent church documentation reaffirms these foundational insights. (*Casti Connubii, Gaudium et Spes, Mulieris Dignitatem, Familiaris Consortio*)

VI. Marriage is the Foundation for the Family

The development of the family is founded upon the mutual exchange of love and support between spouses. The relationship between parents and children is critical in the formation of both an authentically human person and an authentically human society. (*Arcanum, Humanae Vitae, Charter of Rights of the Family, Rite of Marriage, Familiaris Consortio, Christifidelis Laicis*)

VII. The Necessary Integrity of the Purposes of Marriage

Earlier church statements made a stronger emphasis upon the procreative aspect of the marital bond. In contemporary documents the unitive aspect of marriage is explained as the basis for the procreative. While recognizing that both aspects are vital and inseparable, the unitive serves as the foundation for the begetting of a human community. (*Gaudium et Spes, Rite of Marriage, Code of Canon Law 1983*)

VIII. Marriage as Contract and Covenant

The focus on the juridical terms explaining marriage has shifted to a biblical, covenantal language. This is more expressive of the sacramental bond of love between spouses as reflected within the relationship. This covenantal imagery is abundant within the Scriptures as it explains the nature of the relationship between God and Israel. (*Gaudium et Spes, Code of Canon Law 1983, Mulieris Dignitatem, Familiaris Consortio, Rite of Marriage*)

IX. Family as Domestic Church

The domestic church is marked as that originating source in which the love and faith of parents give birth to the life and faith of children. That energizing dynamic between the children and the parents deepens and enriches the graced faith that comes as a gift through marriage. (*Gaudium et Spes, Familiaris Consortio*)

X. Support of Diverse Family Conditions

The response of the church to the specific needs of families in their structure and diversity surfaces in contemporary documents. The critical support given in earlier documents by exhortation now emerges with specific recommendations for pastoral initiatives. Pontifical documents tend to be universal, yet exhort local churches to respond to specific needs and circumstances. (*Familiaris Consortio, Charter of Rights of the Family, Human Life in Our Day, Mixed Marriages*)

XI. Marriage: A Sacrament Among All Baptized Christians

The concept of sacramentality was formerly applied almost exclusively to marriage between Roman Catholics. Prior to Vatican II the advocacy of the sacramental bond among all the baptized began to receive greater attention. This is a critical shift that recognizes that in the very nature of baptism there is the presence of the sacramental grace that enables a sacramental marriage and Christian family. (*Rite of Marriage, Code of Canon Law 1983, Familiaris Consortio*)

XII. Marriage and Family Life as Apostolic

The participation of a Christian family within society is central. The mission of the Church arises within the family as the domestic church. Care and concern for society, which must include political participation and advocacy, emerges from the nature of Christian marriage. (*Rite of Marriage, Gaudium et Spes, Familiaris Consortio*)

XIII. Marriage and Family Life as Ministry

The documents of the past century call for the exercise of a sacramental ministry by both spouses toward one another and within the family. The documents of the last fifty years develop a ministry among family members in which each, according to his or her state in life, is an agent of grace within the family as well as among Christian families. (*Familiaris Consortio, The Rite of Marriage 1969, 1990*)

Arcanum

On Christian Marriage
Pope Leo XIII
February 10, 1880

Major Areas of Concern
- Original unity
- Perpetuity
- Sanctification in Christ
- Indissolubility

This document addresses the original intention of marriage, corrupted by human sin but restored in Christ. It further cites contemporary conflicts between church and state that erode the dignity and purpose of sacramental marriage.

Arcanum is the first of a series of encyclical letters written by successive pontiffs, primarily in reaction to worldwide trends that denied the authority of the Church in marriage. It is important to note that this encyclical was composed prior to the formulation of the universal Code of Canon Law in 1917. The documents that follow *Arcanum* draw heavily upon its reasoning. The rise of socialist and communist philosophies challenged the Church to rearticulate the teaching on marriage and the begetting of children, and to stress that the destruction of the bond of marriage would also result in the ruin of society.

I. **All things made new in Christ is the starting point for a proper understanding of Christian marriage. (§1–3)**

  A. Christianity, as the vehicle of divine revelation, provides the singular source of insight. (§4–5)

  B. The union of man and woman expresses unity and perpetuity, which is the ground for indissolubility. (§5)

II. **The role of sin adversely affects the original condition.**

  A. Corruption of the marital condition occurred by degrees, made evident in the Mosaic permission to divorce. (§6)

  B. Further examples of the breakdown of marital unity in society are noted: polygamy, concubinage, adultery, prostitution, disregard for the begetting of offspring. (§7)

  C. The effects of sin are alleviated through the ministry of Christ. (§8)

III. **The nature of marriage emerges within the body of Scripture and Sacred Tradition, under the authority of God.**

  A. The decrees of Trent regarding marriage are reaffirmed.

  B. The Letter to the Ephesians forms the most substantial biblical base for understanding the sacramentality of marriage. (§9)

  C. Marriage is directed to the propagation of the human race and the faith. (§10)

  D. The spouses have mutual duties and rights:
      1. to cherish mutual love
      2. to be faithful to their marriage vows
      3. to give one another an unfailing and unselfish help
      4. husband is head of the family and wife is called to obedience as a companion. (§11)

  E. Children are to submit and obey parents: parents are bound to the education and virtuous upbringing of children. (§12)

IV. **The role of the Church in marriage has been present to Christians from the beginning of the Church.**

  A. In addressing the competing heresies of both past and present the Church has, through legislation and exhortation, established the clarity of the state of marriage and the mutual dignity of both spouses. (§13–16)

B. Conflicts with civil jurisprudence have led to an extreme that excludes the Church's rights over sacramental marriage. (§17–18)

C. The institution of marriage derives from divine authorship, and the Church has authority to regulate marriage. (§19–23)

V. Sacramental marriage shows forth the nuptial image of Christ and the Church, and is indissoluble. (§24)

A. Human structures add nothing to sacramental marriage. (§25)

B. Marriage is intended for both individual benefit and public welfare, through both the unitive and procreative elements. (§26)

C. The fruits of marriage—holiness, unity, and indissolubility—derive from divine will. (§27)

D. Legislation upholding the natural ends of marriage is critical. (§28–29)

E. Civil divorce is condemned as a moral evil. (§30–32)

F. Opposition to civil divorce is built upon the consistent guardianship of the Church under divine guidance.
  1. Protection of the indissolubility of marriage also safeguards the state. (§33)
  2. The Church has maintained the sanctity of marriage against powerful opposition even in the past, but does not deny the right of lawful authority to establish regulations concerning the civil order of marriage. (§34–35)
  3. The state, using the gift of human reason, needs to draw upon faith and the Church in promoting the public good of the faithful. (§36–38)
  4. An admonition is made to bishops to preserve the doctrine of marriage accurately. (§39)

VI. The Church's teaching on matrimony arises from divine mandate.

A. Because the laws of the state deal with civil concerns, these laws should be known and followed. (§40)

B. The separation of spouses is allowable in extreme cases. Remarriage is an assault against justice unless the first marriage has ended in death. (§41)

C. The virtue of religion properly practiced enables marriage to flourish. (§42)

    D. Great care must be exercised in the case of mixed religion where the faith of the Catholic partner or the proper education of children would be at risk. (§43)

VII. The bishops of the Catholic world are exhorted to minister and provide guidance to married couples in difficulty and to pray for fruitful marriages. (§44–45)

Key Quotes

Let no one be misled by the distinction which supporters of the civil power try to make, whereby they separate the marriage contract from the sacrament so that, leaving the sacramental aspect to the church, the contractual element becomes subject to the power and judgment of the civil power. For there is no basis for such a distinction, or rather such a disruption, since it is clear that in Christian marriage the contract cannot be dissociated from the sacrament; thus there can be no true legitimate contract which is not also a sacrament. For Christ the Lord raised matrimony to the dignity of a sacrament and matrimony is the contract itself provided it is legally made. (§23)

Further, matrimony is a sacrament because it is a sacred and efficient sign of grace and the image of the mystical marriage of Christ with the Church. This image and figure are expressed by the bond of most intimate union by which man and woman bind themselves together, which bond is nothing other than matrimony itself. Hence it is clear that every valid marriage between Christians is, in and of itself, the sacrament; and nothing is further from the truth than to say that the sacrament is a sort of ornament superadded or an extrinsic property that can be dissociated and separated from the contract by the will of men. (§24)

Suggested Readings

Arcanum, S. Kardos in *The New Catholic Encyclopedia*, vol. 1, p. 742.

Arcanum, in Carlen, Claudia, I.H.M. *The Papal Encyclicals* (vols. 1-5). Raleigh, NC: The Pieran Press, 1990. § 81, pp. 29- 40.

[Latin Text: *Acta Leonis*, 2:10-40; *Acta Sanctae Sedis*, 12: 385-402]

Codex Iuris Canonici

The Code of Canon Law
Pope Benedict XV
May 27, 1917

Major Areas of Concern
- Impediments to marriage
- The form of marriage
- Consent in marriage
- The ends of marriage
- Validity of marriage

In 1904 Pius X began the process of preparing a complete and orderly codification of all existing church laws, brought into conformity with contemporary conditions. The code was not promulgated until the reign of Benedict XV. The sections on marriage focus on marriage by its nature being a sacred contract. They hold that the primary end of marriage is the procreation and education of children and that the secondary end is mutual support and the allaying of concupiscence. One hundred thirty-one canons are applied to the sacrament of matrimony. The impediments to a sacramental marriage and the basis for valid consent are extensively reviewed.

The 1917 code made no attempt to present a theological vision or definition for sacramental marriage. Canonical commentators subsequent to the code made several attempts at such a definition but among them there was no consensus. The code, derived from the decrees of Trent, nonetheless reflects the sociological understanding of the late nineteenth and early twentieth centuries.

I. Marriage: General Provisions: Preliminaries: Impediments (cc. 1012–1057)

A. General Provisions (cc. 1012–1016)
1. Preliminaries (cc. 1017–1034)
2. Impediments in General (cc. 1035–1057)

II. Particular Impediments (cc. 1058–1080)

A. Impeding Impediments (cc. 1058–1066) [illicit yet valid marriages]

B. Diriment Impediments (cc. 1067–1080) [invalidating]

III. Matrimonial Consent: The Form of Marriage: Other Provisions (cc. 1081–1117)

A. Matrimonial Consent (cc. 1081–1093)

B. The Form of Marriage, etc. (cc. 1094–1107)

C. Other Provisions (cc. 1108–1117)

IV. Dissolution, Separation, Convalidation (cc. 1118–1143)

A. Dissolution of the Bond (cc. 1118–1127)

B. Separation (cc. 1128–1132)

C. Simple Convalidation (cc. 1133–1137)

D. *Sanatio in Radice*, etc. (cc. 1138–1143)

Key Quotes

Christ our Lord elevated the very contract of marriage between baptized persons to the dignity of a sacrament. (c. 1012.1)

Therefore it is impossible for a valid contract of marriage between baptized persons to exist without being by that very fact a sacrament. (c. 1012.2)

The primary end of marriage is the procreation and education of children; its secondary end is mutual help and the allaying of concupiscence. (c. 1013.1)

The essential properties of marriage are unity and indissolubility, which acquire a peculiar firmness in Christian marriage by reason of its sacrament character. (c. 1013.2)

Suggested Readings

Bouscaren, T. Lincoln, and Ellis, Adam C. *Canon Law: A Text and Commentary.* Milwaukee: The Bruce Publishing Company, 1957 (3rd ed.).

Häring, Bernard. *The Law of Christ.* (3 Vols.) Westminster, MD: Newman, 1963.

Mathis, M., and Bonner, D. *The Pastoral Companion: A Handbook of Canon Law.* (14th ed.) Chicago: Franciscan Herald Press, 1976.

Wrenn, Lawrence. *Annulments.* (4th ed. rev.) Washington, D.C.: Canon Law Society of America, 1983.

Casti Connubii

On Christian Marriage
Pope Pius XI
December 31, 1930

Major Areas of Concern
- Grounds for marriage
- Procreation
- Children
- The limits of civil law
- Divorce
- Human freedom

This encyclical builds upon Leo XIII's *Arcanum,* published fifty years earlier. Pius XI rejects the position that marriage is merely a private affair and restates Augustine's three goods of marriage (children, conjugal fidelity, and the sacrament). Pius XI presents the dignity and obligations of parenthood and the absolute unity and indissolubility of marriage. He addresses several current threats against these goods, including divorce, birth control, abortion, sterilization, adultery, and cohabitation.

The events of World War I and the subsequent great worldwide economic depression helped socialist and communist philosophies to gain dominance, particularly in Europe, in the years following the pontificates of Pius X and Benedict XV. Neither Pius X nor Benedict XV addressed substantial teaching on marriage and family. This encyclical is among the longest and most critical efforts of Pius XI. Fully half of the document responds to pressing challenges of this time.

I. An exhortation on the dignity and divine institution of marriage is given. (§1–4)

A. The errors of the day against the divine institution of marriage are presented. (§5–7)

B. The nature of the marriage contract is explained.
   1. Human freedom allows one to choose to marry. (§8)
   2. Though marriage is divinely instituted human beings are the authors of a particular marriage. (§9)

II. The blessings of marriage are presented. (§10)

A. Children are the first of the blessings of marriage. (§11–12)
   1. Christian parents are destined to raise offspring to be members of the household of God. (§13)
   2. Personal sanctification is critical for Christian spouses in the generation of the life of grace of their children. (§14–15)

B. The proper education of children is the principal right and duty of both parents. Only in the unity provided by sacramental marriage is this possible. (§16)
   1. The primary end of marriage is the procreation and education of children. (§17)
   2. Procreation of offspring outside of marriage is forbidden for the good of children. (§18)

III. Conjugal honor (mutual fidelity) completes marriage. (§19)

A. In Christ, marriage is restored to its original capacity for human fulfillment. (§20)

B. Marital chastity and conjugal love are essential for the formation and perfection of spousal love. (§21–25)

C. Family life comes from the order of love between spouses, including a specific ordering of the spouses. (§26)
   1. Human liberty is enriched through mutual submission in the order of love. This mutual love is sacrificial action. (§27–29)
   2. Elements composing the blessings of marriage are: unity, chastity, charity, honorable obedience, indissolubility—which is the pivotal note of the sacrament. (§30–33)
   3. By divine right, a perpetual bond exists in every true marriage and is beyond the control of merely civil law. (§34–36)

D. Benefits arise from indissolubility. (§37)
   1. Every valid marriage between baptized persons is a sacramen-

tal marriage. Valid matrimonial consent constitutes the sign of grace. (§38–40)

E. Sacrament bestows sanctifying grace assisting the couple to perform those duties that constitute the married life. (§41–43)

IV. **Contemporary problems are adversely affecting sacramental marriage. (§44–46)**

A. The source of these evils lies in the denial of the divine foundation of marriage and reducing the married life to a merely secular institution. (§47–50)

B. Cohabitation is morally unacceptable, going contrary to the nature of an authentically stable union. (§51–52)

C. Contraception goes contrary to the good of offspring. Frustration of the marriage act by any form contrary to nature is morally wrong. (§53–56)

D. Pastors and confessors in the name of the Church are to correct with compassion false understandings about birth control. (§57–60)

V. **Considerations on divine and civil law are clarified.**

A. No difficulty justifies the use of acts that are contrary to the law of God, specifically direct abortion. (§61–66)

B. Civil legislation is bound to protect the innocent. It is restricted by the nature of the family and parenthood in its exercise of authority. This refers specifically to recourse to abortion or sterilization. (§67–70)

C. The rights of private individuals exclude surgical mutilation, except when the good of the whole body requires it. (§71)

VI. **Concepts destructive of conjugal trust are specified and condemned.**

A. Sins committed against the good of offspring become in some way a sin against conjugal love. (§72)

B. Adultery is always forbidden. (§73)

C. The dignity of women cannot include any excessive idea of liberty that erodes family life. (§74–75)

D. The equality of spousal rights is grounded in the dignity of the human person and inseparable from the marital bond. (§76)

E. Civil legislation that recognizes the social and economic condition of the married woman and the welfare of the family needs to be promoted. (§77)

F. Matrimony is no mere secular or psychological state. The religious dimension of human life needs to be emphasized in society. (§78–79)

VII. The divine basis for Christian marriage is reaffirmed.
A. God is the author of marriage, and its religious character is made most clear in the Christian sacrament. (§80–81)
 1. Strong caution and prohibitions against mixed marriages among Christians are explained. (§82)
 2. The danger of religious indifference resulting from mixed religions is emphasized. (§83–84)

B. Rationale against civil divorce is specified.
 1. The contemporary grounds for civil divorce analyzed without recourse to divine institution of marriage are inadequate. (§85–86)
 2. The scriptural ground against divorce, even in the case of adultery, is reaffirmed as divine law. (§87–88)
 3. Conditions for separation are stated. The emphasis upon the stability of the family unit for mutual benefit of spouses and children is affirmed. (§89–90)
 4. Since divorce undermines the well being of the family and its members, it is ultimately degrading to society. (§91–92)

C. Remedies for the preservation and nurturing of sacramental marriage are presented.
 1. A return to the original state of the divine plan for marriage is critical. (§93–96)
  a. The chief obstacle in human relationship is an unbridled lust. (§97)
  b. The conversion of the individual, prayer for divine grace, and celebration of the sacraments are presented as critical to restoration of sacramental marriage. (§98–101)
 2. Private moral judgment must give way to faithful obedience to the authoritative teachings of the Church of Christ in these matters. (§102–104)

D. The content of premarital instructions is summarized.

    1. Instruction of the faithful about marriage is critical for the foundation of sacramental marriage. (§105–107)

       a. Wholesome instruction going beyond a merely physical presentation is required. (§108)

       b. The teaching of Christ must be preserved in its entirety in presenting marriage instructions. (§109)

    2. The determination on the part of the spouses to observe the divine law regarding marriage is essential. (§110–111)

    3. The preparation for sacramental marriage is both remote and proximate. (§112)

       a. The role of parents in providing a solid example of faithful Christian love is irreplaceable. (§113–114)

       b. Most appropriate to the proximate preparation of a good married life is the choice of a spouse; prudent parental advice is needed. (§114–115)

    4. Economic considerations are an important aspect in providing for marital and family stability. (§116–118)

       a. The care for the poor should be a consideration in marital instruction. (§119)

       b. Rights of the family and the obligations of the state are strongly emphasized. (§120–121)

E. Access to state assistance for children must be provided to all women and their children. (§122)

F. Laws that promote sound marital development and solid family life are to be fostered both by civil and religious authority. (§123–125)

    1. The Lateran Pact is cited as an example of this. (§126–127)

VIII. Concluding Exhortation and Apostolic Benediction given. (§128–130)

Key Quote

But although matrimony by nature is of divine institution, yet the human will has a part, and a very important part, to play in it. Each marriage, in so far as it is a conjugal union between a particular man and a particular woman, arises solely out of a free consent of the two partners; and this free act by which each yields and receives the specifically marital right is so necessary for the constitution of marriage that it cannot be supplied by any human power. But the only role of this human freedom is to decide that each of the partners in fact wished to enter the state of matrimony, and to marry this particular person. The freedom of man has no power whatever over the nature of matrimony itself, and, therefore, when once a person has contracted marriage, he becomes subject to its essential laws and properties. (§6)

Suggested Readings

Casti Connubii. S. Kardos in *The New Catholic Encyclopedia,* vol. 3, p. 190.

Casti Connubii, in Carlen, Claudia, I.H.M. *The Papal Encyclicals* (vols. 1-5). Raleigh, NC: The Pieran Press, 1990, §209, pp. 391-414. [An extensive list of readings is provided here.]

Thomas, J.L., S.J. *The Catholic Viewpoint On Marriage and the Family.* Garden City, NY: Doubleday, 1958.

[Latin text: *Acta Apostolica Sedes* 22 (1930), 339-92; amended text, 604]

Vegliare Con Sollecitudine

Address to the Catholic Union of Midwives
Pope Pius XII
October 29, 1951

Major Areas of Concern
- The apostolate of midwifery
- God and humankind bringing about human life
- Defense of the human person
- Inviolability of the unborn
- Professional competence

The significance of the public audiences of the popes of the latter part of the twentieth century needs to be acknowledged. Pius XII stands as a transitional figure in many ways. His incorporation of the media of radio, motion pictures, and television shows a clear appreciation of twentieth-century advances in communication. Pius XII's use of papal audiences and addresses to publicly present the Church's teaching began a trend continued by successive pontiffs. This discourse articulates the Church's concerns for the dignity of the human person in the face of advancing technological abilities. Although not an encyclical, this speech stands as the forerunner of *Humanae Vitae* and *Donum Vitae*. Pope Pius exhorts Catholic midwives to inspire personal confidence and show professional skill in upholding the sacredness of human life. In addition, midwives are exhorted to assist the mother in her role and to do this with great generosity.

I. Greeting and Welcome to Midwives (¶258)

A. The function of midwives is to assist in the parents' collaboration with God in the creation of new life. (¶259)

   1. The order of the creator is clear and embraces both external action and the internal human will. Humans have a duty to uphold this natural order as it touches the evolution of life. (¶260–261)

   2. Professional training enables one to know the course of nature and its laws. An informed conscience is essential to good moral action. (¶262)

II. Some Specific Considerations

A. Each profession willed by God has an apostolic purpose. (¶263)

   1. Personal influence and professional competence is how midwives advance the moral and religious value for human life. (¶264–267)

   2. The religious faith of a professional is the foundation standing against unethical claims. (¶268)

   3. Moral guidance and authority are presented through the genuine humanity and Christian life of a professional. (¶269)

B. Zealous promotion of human life is the second aspect of the apostolate. (¶270)

   1. Midwifery allows the testimony of "mind, heart, and facts" to demonstrate the real value of human life. (¶271)

   2. Every human life, from the moment of conception, is sacred; no direct violation of that life is morally acceptable. (¶272)

   3. The apostolate demands one to be prepared to resolutely defend and protect when possible the unborn life. (¶273–274)

   4. The child is given to the care of both parents and the role of the father needs to be honored. (¶275)

   5. Midwives are strongly encouraged to support the mother in her vocation. (¶276)

   6. Childbirth and motherhood affirm the essential dignity of the woman and are a means to salvation. This needs to be affirmed. (¶277–278)

   7. Openness to the "blessings of new life" must always be honored and never derided. (¶279)

   8. Baptism is the gateway to supernatural life. The Church's concern about the baptism of infants in cases of serious danger is easily understood. (¶280–282)

C. Assisting the mother in marital life is a third task. (¶283)

    1. The motherhood of Mary is exalted. (¶284)

    2. Conjugal loving calls for maternal loving. (¶285)

    3. The encouragement of maternal and conjugal love is an urgent objective of the apostolate. (¶286)

        a. In the face of many fears, cultivating an appreciation for new life among the spouses is an important role. (¶287)

        b. One may not accede to requests contrary to childbirth in this regard. This is contrary to natural and divine law. (¶288–289)

        c. Midwives are exhorted to follow this course.

    4. Direct sterilization to render childbearing impossible is a grave disorder and cannot be encouraged in any case. No public agency has moral authority in this matter. (¶291)

        a. Midwives are called to oppose such tendencies. (¶292)

        b. Midwives are called to be well informed but cautious about promoting the recourse to periods of natural sterility in marriage. (¶293–294)

        c. An appreciation of moral law is critical here. (¶295)

    5. Two hypotheses are presented.

        a. There is nothing adverse to the exercise of full conjugal relations even during infertile period.

        b. There is a moral problem when conjugal relations are restricted exclusively to the infertile period. (¶296)

    6. Marital consent is doubtful in those cases where the intention exists from the beginning to restrict conjugal relationships to the infertile period. (¶297)

        a. The good will of the partners in restricting conjugal acts to infertile periods does not guarantee the validity of marital consent. (¶298)

        b. Conjugal duties may be withheld by spouses in the face of sufficient grave reasons. (¶299)

            i. The goal of offspring, which benefits societies, cannot be evaded without serious cause. (¶300)

        c. Serious medical, genetic, economic, and social reasons can exempt a married couple from conjugal obligations and can legitimate the use of the infertile period for a long duration, even for the entirety of the marriage. (¶301)

        d. Midwives are asked to consider their professional role in assisting such couples in decision making. (¶302)

            i. Medical judgments are within midwives' competence.

Non-medical judgments advocating positions contrary to Church teaching should be corrected.

ii. In extreme cases complete abstinence should be promoted and not regarded as impossible in the face of divine grace. (¶303–305)

    a. Heroic virtue is to be encouraged as necessary in extreme cases and as possible in contemporary marriage. (¶306)

iii. The apostolate of midwives is directed to the service of the family and the positive vision of motherhood. (¶307)

7. This Apostolate and the Defense of Human Dignity.

a. Sexual intercourse expresses and brings about personal and affective union. (¶309)

i. The contemporary expression of "personalist" theories is reviewed with caution; they relativize the good of offspring. (¶310–311)

    a. The person of the offspring needs to be affirmed and supported in this apostolate. (¶312)

    b. The primary and secondary ends of marriage need to be understood and presented accurately: personalist ends are subordinated. (¶313)

        1. Prior papal statements have corrected this faulty opinion. (¶314)

        2. The good of the persons arising from the communion of married life is willed by God and inseparable from the primary good of marriage. (¶315–316)

        3. Conjugal acts are not merely biological but consist of personal cooperation that expresses a mutual self-donation. (¶317–318)

        4. Where this mutual exchange is permanently impossible, from the onset the object of the marriage contract is null. (¶319)

        5. The task of midwives includes presenting the correct scale of values in marriage; personalist ends are secondary. (¶320)

    c. The renunciation of a conjugal life does not demean human dignity. (¶321)

        1. Midwives need to instill right order of values in support of generativity. (¶322–323)

8. Human Dignity and Generativity
  a. Conjugal rights and sensual pleasure are intended by God. (¶325)
    i. Sexual relations are bound to marriage and to its purposes. (¶326)
    ii. The unrestrained surrender to sexual passions, though promoted by many, is contrary to the plan of God. (¶327–331)
    iii. Marital happiness derives from mutual respect, not sexual pleasure. (¶332)
  b. Midwives need to reaffirm the link between sexual pleasure and the service of life both personally and professionally. (¶333)
  c. The affirmation of these teachings is a pressing duty in defense of Christian marriage and the personal dignity of the spouse. (¶334–335)

III. Conclusion

A. This profession sets forth a valuable service of action and guidance; it requires top-notch medical information and deep religious conviction. (¶336–337)

B. The apostolic blessing is given. (¶338)

Key Quote

The Creator in His goodness and wisdom has willed to make use of the work of the man and the woman to preserve and propagate the human race, by joining them in wedlock. The same creator has arranged that the husband and wife find pleasure and happiness of mind and body in the performance of that function. Consequently, the husband and wife do no wrong in seeking out and enjoying this pleasure. They are accepting what the creator intended for them. (¶326)

If the exclusive aim of nature, or at least, its primary aim, had been the mutual giving and possessing of husband and wife in joy and delight: if nature had arranged that act only to make their personal experience happy in the highest possible degree, and not as an incentive in the service of life, then the creator would have made use of another plan in the formation and constitution of the natural act. (¶328)

Suggested Readings

A Positive Vision for Family Life: A Resource Guide for Pope John Paul II's Apostolic Exhortation Familiaris Consortio. Ed. by Rev. Thomas Lynch and Valerie Dillon. Commission on Marriage and Family Life. Department of Education, USCC, 1985.

Albacete, Lorenzo M. *Commentary on Instruction on Respect for Human Life in its Origin and on the Dignity of Procreation*. Boston: St. Paul Editions, 1987.

Hogan, Richard M., and LeVoir, John M. *Covenant of Love: Pope John Paul II on Sexuality, Marriage, and Family in the Modern World*. (reprinted) San Francisco: Ignatius Press, 1986.

Liebard, Odile M. *Official Catholic Teachings: Love and Sexuality*. Wilmington, NC: Consortium Books, 1978.

Wojtyla, K. (John Paul II). *Reflections on Humanae Vitae: Conjugal Morality and Spirituality*. Boston: St. Paul Editions, 1984.

[Latin text: *Acta Apostolica Sedes* 43 (1951), 835-54]

Nell'Ordine Della

Address to the Association of Larger Families
Pope Pius XII
November 26, 1951

Major Areas of Concern
- The dignity of human life
- The equal dignity of mother and child
- The endurance of the family in the modern world
- The role of the sacraments

This document follows the global conflicts of the early twentieth century. Although Pius XII issued no encyclicals in the area of marriage and family, this document contains the seeds of many subsequent papal statements. Speaking to the Association of Larger Families, Pius XII reaffirms the Church's support for their mission. He clarifies the teaching of the Church on the dignity of human life from the moment of conception and restates the condemnation of killing those judged useless by others.

I. Family is the most precious natural social institution.

   A. Matrimony is the root of the family.

   B. The Church in every age is the powerful advocate of inviolable family rights and liberty. (§340)

      1. The threefold aim of the large family movement is to:

        a. influence family policy legislation

---

b. promote solidarity between families

c. advance the Christian culture of the family. (§341)

2. Popes have frequently advocated the protection of families from serious dangers.

   a. God's grace and heroic efforts are necessary to heal the damage left by both world wars.

      i. Overpopulation, the wars, and self-interest contribute to the crisis in housing.

      ii. Legislators and social workers should find remedies. (§342)

   b. Establishing a sufficient family wage frees the mother from the necessity of working outside the home.

      i. This promotes a fitting family atmosphere. (§343)

      ii. The family cannot be reduced to existing solely for the service of society. (§344)

3. Over the years, a consistent teaching on conjugal morality has been taught even while being severely challenged by society. (§345–346)

   a. Matrimony is the center of this doctrine.

   b. "The direct attack on human life, as a means to an end—in the present case to the end of saving another life is illicit." (§347)

   c. Preservation from direct voluntary assault is a fundamental right of innocent human life from the very beginning of that life and across all the stages of development. (§348)

   d. Attempting to save both lives is morally imperative; both are of equal dignity. (§349) Where the mother's death is certain, and she desires the life in the womb to be preserved, preserve it. (§350)

   e. As none can be certain as to whose life is more precious, presenting the life of the mother as superior to that of the unborn child is illicit.

      i. Judgments about innocent life stand independent of that life's function. (§351)

   f. The expressions direct attempt and direct killing are deliberate.

      i. Some therapeutic procedures may result in the certain death of a child, even when not directly intended. (§352)

      ii. One needs to consider the gravity of the medical condition, other available and effective treatments, and if the procedure can be postponed until after birth. (§353)

  g. The legitimacy and very wide limits of controlling births are once again affirmed. Medical research is encouraged in this area. (§354)

  h. Lively faith and frequent reception of the sacraments are the most powerful aids in married life.

4. Natural strength and the grace of matrimony assist us in the present age and enable the married to overcome all trials. (§355)

Key Quote

Innocent human life, in whatever condition it may be, from the first moment of its existence, is to be preserved from any direct voluntary attack. This is a fundamental right of the human person, of general value in the Christian concept of life; valid for both the still hidden life in the womb and for the newborn babe, and opposed to direct abortion as it is to the direct killing of the child before, during, and after birth. (§348)

Suggested Readings

[Latin Text: *Acta Apostolica Sedes* 43 (1951), 855-60]

Vatican Council II

In contrast to earlier papal encyclicals and statements, the Second Vatican Council takes on a strong personalistic framework for its discussion of marriage and family. In *Lumen Gentium* (§11) the ecclesial nature of the sacrament of marriage is explained, with the family being called "the domestic church." Marriage is recognized as a path to holiness, and in the document *Gaudium et Spes* the ends of marriage are given equal status with the recognition that mutual love and procreation are intimately linked together.

The emphasis in these documents on the vocation of marriage and family reflects a newfound optimism and openness toward the world. The dramatic shift in emphasis to a spirituality focused on one's state in life is seen in the *Pastoral Constitution on the Church* and reflected on the understanding of marriage and family.

There are many adequate historical surveys of Vatican II and its teachings. Please consult these works, listed among the suggested readings, for a clearer historical map.

I. Gaudium et Spes (*Pastoral Constitution on the Church in the Modern World*), December 7, 1965
   A. Conjugal love is central to the Christian's married life and serves as the basis for healthy families. (§47)

B. Conjugal love is sanctifying and redemptive.
   1. Parents have a central role in the family's spiritual formation.
   2. Children contribute to parents' holiness. Families share spirituality with one another. (§48)

C. There is a radical call to holiness in the Christian's married life.
   1. Genuine conjugal love will lead couples to work for social change.
   2. We must prepare couples well for marriage. (§49)

D. Couples should cooperate with their Creator in the creation of new life.
   1. Couples "in reverence for the good of society have the task of" transmitting life and educating children. (§50)

E. From the moment of conception, new life must be guarded.
   1. We must harmonize conjugal love with responsible transmission of life determined by objective standards. (§51)

F. The family is a "school of deeper humanity."
   1. Parents, especially fathers, should actively participate in the education of their children.
   2. The rights of parents to have and educate children should be safeguarded in society. (§52)

II. Gravissimum Educationis *(Declaration on Christian Education)*, October 28, 1965

A. Parents are the primary educators of their children.

B. Society should assist and support families in this role. (§3)

III. Lumen Gentium *(Dogmatic Constitution on the Church)*, November 21, 1964

A. Christian married couples attain holiness through their married life and in the rearing and education of their children.

B. Parents, by word and example, preach their faith. (§11)

C. Christian family life is prophetic. (§35)

D. The mutual support of Christian married couples builds up the life of charity. (§41)

IV. Apostolicam Actuositatem *(Decree on the Apostolate of the Laity)*, November 18, 1965

A. The apostolate of married persons and families is crucial in the Church and society.
   1. Couples should work in society to promote just legislation and policies for couples and families.
   2. Families evangelize each other through their care of one another and those in need. (§11)

B. Family life is the basis for the laity's formation in mission and ministry in the Church.
   1. Children's education in their church and community is essential. Parents should actively promote this formation, with the assistance of the clergy. (§30)

Key Quotes

Christian spouses, in virtue of the sacrament of matrimony, signify and share in the mystery of that union and fruitful love which exists between Christ and the Church (cf. Eph 5:32). They help each other to attain to holiness in their married life and by the rearing and education of their children. And thus, in their state and way of life they have their own special gift among the people of God (cf. 1 Cor 7:7). For their union gives rise to a family where new citizens are born to human society, and in baptism they are made into children of God by the Grace of the Holy Spirit, for the perpetuation of God's people throughout the centuries. Within the family, which is, so to speak, "the domestic church," the parents should be first to preach the faith to their children by word and example .... (*Lumen Gentium*, §11)

The intimate partnership of life and conjugal love has been established by the creator and provided by him with its own laws. It has its beginning in the marriage covenant, that is, in an irrevocable personal consent. Thus, from the human act by which the spouses mutually give and accept each other, there arises also in the eyes of society, that institution whose firmness stems from God's disposition... Man and woman, who by the marriage covenant "are no longer two but one" (Mt 19:6), render one another help and service by the intimate union of their persons and activities. They experience a sense of their oneness, and deepen it day by day. Being a mutual self gift of two persons, this intimate union demands, as indeed does the good of the children, the complete fidelity of the spouses, and their indissoluble unity. (*Gaudium et Spes,* §48)

Suggested Readings

Commentary on the Documents of Vatican II. vols. I-V New York: Herder and Herder, 1969. [An extensive historical review of each document with a commentary.]

See the Commentaries on each Vatican document in *The Documents of Vatican II,* ed. by Walter M. Abbott, S.J. New York: America Press, 1966.

Matrimonii Sacramentum

Instruction on Mixed Marriages
Sacred Congregation for the Doctrine of the Faith
March 18, 1966

Matrimonia Mixta

Apostolic Letter
on Mixed Marriages
January 7, 1970

Major Areas of Concern
- Mixed religion
- Interfaith couples
- Marriage ceremonies
- Pastoral care
- Children

The Church's growing concern for ecumenical relationships, resulting in Vatican II's *Decree on Ecumenism*, found a tangible expression for implementation in the sacrament of marriage. *Matrimonii Sacramentum* and *Matrimonia Mixta* are examples of the Church's application of these ecumenical principles. While retaining the important role of the Catholic partner within a marriage between baptized Christians, these two documents show a much more supportive attitude toward mixed marriages. Christian/Non-Christian marriages, though unable to be accounted as a sacrament, are given pastoral support.

I. Matrimonii Sacramentum

    A. Church has the obligation to guard the faith of the married couple. (¶1)

        1. Two impediments to mixed marriages in canon law are noted: mixed religion and disparity of cult. (¶2)

        1. Local ordinaries can dispense from these impediments with good cause. (¶11)

        2. Pastors should express the Church's concern about mixed marriage to those marrying a non-Catholic Christian. (¶3)

        3. The Church recognizes our changing society and the possibility of more couples entering mixed marriages. (¶4–5)

        4. Supporting the Church's teaching on the sanctity of marriage is a priority, especially when presenting teaching about the ends of marriage to engaged couples. (¶6–9)

        5. Church laws about marriage should be reviewed, as they are affected by the Vatican Council II *Decree on Ecumenism*. (¶10)

        6. Vatican II acknowledged this concern. (¶11)

    B. During the preparation process for marriage, engaged couples should be informed of their obligations in the area of mixed marriages.

        1. It is the parish priest's obligation to emphasize that safeguarding the faith of the Catholic partner and children is necessary. (¶13–14)

        2. The non-Catholic partner should be informed of the Catholic teaching on the unity and indissolubility of marriage and the obligation on the Catholic partner to baptize and educate children in the faith. (¶15–16)

        3. The Catholic should promise in writing to abide by this commitment, and the non-Catholic partner should also be asked to verbally agree to this. (¶17–18)

            a. In certain circumstances the local ordinary can dispense from this obligation, with good reason being shown. (¶19–20)

    C. The canonical form for mixed marriages must be observed. (¶21–22)

        1. When a non-Catholic minister participates in the marriage celebration, only one rite can be used, with the minister participating (e.g., through reading of prayers or through a word of congratulations). (¶23–24)

    D. Practical supports for mixed marriages should be provided at the local level. (¶25)

E. Prior law on excommunication if one marries before non-Catholic minister is abolished; ecumenical efforts encouraged. (¶26–29)

F. Catholics should share their faith by example with their non-Catholic spouses and their children. (¶30)

II. Matrimonia Mixta

A. Mixed marriages have been and continue to need careful attention. (¶1)
   1. Mixed marriages are a consequence of division among Christians. (¶1)
   2. Difficulties are implicit in a mixed marriage. (¶2)
   3. The Church is aware that couples have a natural right to marry, but it has discouraged mixed marriages. (¶3)
   4. Care for children and their faith development is needed. Pastoral care, especially with an unbaptized person marrying a Catholic, is necessary. (¶4)
   5. In doctrine and law a marriage between a Catholic and unbaptized person is not the same as that between a Catholic and baptized non-Catholic. (¶5)
   6. Between two baptized persons there is a "true sacrament" with all spiritual benefits, unlike that between a baptized and a non-baptized person. (¶6)
   7. Even so, there can be differences, especially in the area of morality and Church teaching. (¶7)

B. The Catholic is bound by Church teaching and discipline. (¶8–9)
   1. Children should be baptized and educated in the faith. (¶10–11)
   2. The form of the wedding can be adapted to the situation. Pastoral care to married couples of mixed faith is also needed. (¶12, 32)
   3. The prior instruction (*Matrimonii Sacramentum*) and this document will assist in the development of the future code of canon law. (¶14–15)
   4. Eastern Catholic marriages to non-baptized are not subject to these norms. (¶16)
   5. Canonical law should affirm the spirit of the decrees of Vatican II on ecumenical concerns (¶17) especially:
      a. Where there is a mixed marriage (Catholic/non-Catholic), dispensation by the ordinary or their delegate is necessary. (¶18, 20)

      b. Marriages by Catholic and unbaptized without dispensation are invalid. (¶19)

      c. A promise by the Catholic party to have the child baptized and raised in the Catholic Church is needed. (¶21)

      d. At an appropriate time, the non-Catholic partner needs to be informed of this promise. (¶22)

      e. The ends and essential properties of marriage should be reviewed with the engaged couple. (¶23)

C. Local conferences of bishops are responsible for implementation. (¶24, 25, 28, 30)

D. Local ordinaries have the right to dispense from the canonical form in any mixed marriages. All validly contracted marriages must be included in the marriage register. (¶26, 27, 29, 33, 34, 35)

    1. Only one ceremony with one minister presiding is allowed.

Key Quote

Local ordinaries and parish priests shall see to it that the Catholic husband or wife and the children born of a mixed marriage do not lack spiritual assistance in fulfilling their duties of conscience. They shall encourage the Catholic husband or wife to keep ever in mind the divine gift of the Catholic faith and bear witness to it with gentleness and reverence, and with a clear conscience. (*Matrimonia Mixta*, ¶32)

Suggested Readings

Lawler, Michael. *Ecumenical Marriage and Remarriage: Gifts and Challenges to the Churches.* Mystic, CT: Twenty-Third Publications, 1990.

[*Matrimonii Sacramentum*, Latin Text: *Acta Apostolica Sedes* 58 (1966), 235–239; *Matrimonia Mixta*, Latin Text: *Acta Apostolica Sedes* 62 (1970), 257-263]

Humanae Vitae

On the Regulation of Birth
Pope Paul VI
July 25, 1968

Major Areas of Concern
- Marital love
- Teaching authority of Church
- Responsible parenthood
- Priority of natural law
- Integrity of family life

Humanae Vitae reflects the concerns of the Church on issues of population distribution and marital life. It provides a rationale for the Church's long-standing recognition of the procreative end of marriage and develops the theme of the unitive nature of the conjugal act as essential to marriage. Composed in 1968, this document became the center of controversy on issues of theological dissent and personal conscience. The document reaffirms the natural law basis for its teaching against contraceptive methods of birth control. It also applies personalist considerations as it promotes the unitive dimension of marital love.

I. The Teaching Authority of the Church

A. Rapid development of population centers is a challenge to society worldwide. (§2)

B. Dominion over the forces of nature has led humankind to apply scientific principles to all aspects of human life. This gives rise to new questions. (§3)

C. The teaching authority of the Church is grounded within the mandate of Christ. (§4)

D. Consciousness of the role of the authority brought forth in a special commission of experts to study questions, but without consensus of judgment. Ultimate judgment in this matter resides in the office of the Pontiff. (§5–6)

II. Doctrinal Principles

A. The question of human procreation cannot be limited to mere scientific analysis. (§7)

B. Marriage derives its dignity from God and is that state of life within which husband and wife perfect each other with God's grace. (§8)

C. Characteristics of marital love are four: fully human, total gift, faithful and exclusive, and fecund. (§9)

D. Responsible parenthood has to be considered in its complexity. It requires that husband and wife keep a right order of priorities as regards their own duties to God, themselves, their families, and society. They are bound to do what corresponds to the will of God. (§10)

E. The intimacy of sexual activity is bound by the course of natural law. (§11)

F. The fundamental nature of the marriage act, while uniting husband and wife, renders them capable of generating new life. (§12)

G. Conjugal acts must be mutually and freely entered into and must further reflect the capacity to transmit life. (§13)

H. Unlawful birth control methods are: direct abortion, direct sterilization, and any act directly intended to prevent procreation as a means or end. (§14)

I. Lawful means of birth regulation include recourse to infertile periods of cycle as well as therapeutic means necessary to remedy diseases. (§15, 16)

J. The consequences of artificial methods include marital infidelity, diminished moral sensitivity, debasement of spouse, and imposition of public authority within fertility issues. (§17)

K. The Church's concern is proclaiming dignity of sacrament and human persons. (§18)

III. Pastoral Directives

A. Church proposes these directives as a mother and teacher of all peoples. (§19)

B. The following directives are indicated: the observing of divine law, the necessity of self-discipline, and chastity between spouses. (§20–22)

C. Authentic solutions require responses of public authorities, scientists, physicians and nurses, and Christian couples. (§23–27)

D. Christian witness and pastoral care require the diligence of Christian faithful, priests, and bishops. (§28–30)

Key Quote

This doctrine, often set forth by the teaching authority, is founded upon the inseparable connection, willed by God, and which man cannot break on his own initiative, between the two meanings of the conjugal act: union and procreation. For, by its intimate structure, the conjugal act, while most closely uniting the spouses, enables them to procreate new lives according to laws inscribed in the very being of man and woman. It is by safeguarding these two essential aspects, union and procreation, that the conjugal act preserves in its fullness the sense of true mutual love and its ordination towards man's most high calling to parenthood. We believe that the men of our day are particularly capable of understanding the deeply reasonable and human character of this fundamental principle. (§12)

Suggested Readings

Ford, John C., S.J., et al. *The Teaching of "Humanae* Vitae": *A Defense.* San Francisco: Ignatius Press, 1988.

Humanae Vitae, in Carlen, Claudia, I.H.M. *The Papal Encyclicals* (vols. 1–5). Raleigh, NC: The Pieran Press, 1990, no. 277, pp. 223-236.

McCarthy, Donald G. and Bayer, Edward J. *Handbook On Critical Sexual Issues.* Garden City, NY: Doubleday and Co. Image Books, 1984.

Mulligan, James J. *The Pope and the Theologians: The Humanae Vitae Controversy.* Mount St. Mary's Seminary Press, Emmitsburg, MD, 1968.

Smith, Janet E. *Humanae Vitae: A Generation Later.* Washington, D.C.: The Catholic University of America, 1991.

Von Hildebrand, Dietriech. *The Encyclical Humanae Vitae: A Sign of Contradiction.* Chicago: Franciscan Herald Press, 1969.

Wojtyla, K. (John Paul II) *Fruitful and Responsible Love.* New York: Seabury Press, 1979.

Wojtyla, K. (John Paul II). *Reflections on Humanae Vitae: Conjugal Morality and Spirituality.* Boston: St. Paul Editions, 1984.

[Latin Text: *Acta Apostolica Sedes* 60 (1968), 487-503.]

Human Life
in Our Day

National Conference of Catholic Bishops
November 15, 1968

Major Areas of Concern
- Christian family
- Responsible parenthood
- Conscience formation
- Norms of theological dissent

This statement responds to concerns about U.S. attitudes toward abortion and war and the recently published encyclical *Humanae Vitae*. The U.S. bishops speak out in defense of *Humanae Vitae* and provide a pastoral rationale to support spouses and families during a time of great upheaval in American society and in the Church.

The first half of this document (to paragraph 92) provides a response to the theological debate on the birth control issue in the broader context of Vatican II's teaching on marriage and family. The second section of the document is a response to the concerns about war in a society in conflict over the Vietnam war.

I. Introduction

  A. The defense of life provides the ground for dialogue between the believing community and humanists on their concerns for both life and peace. (§1–8)

---

1. The focus of this pastoral letter is the maturing of family life in a peaceful world order. (§9)

II. The Christian Family

A. One's attitude toward life shapes the person. As the Church is the family of God, so it is concerned for the human family and is committed to doctrinal defense of and practical witness to family life. (§10–11)

B. The Church's teachings on marriage go beyond strict sociological and cultural analysis and cultural values. (§12)

C. One's family reinforces fidelity to life and hope and is the place where God's image is reproduced in the world. (§13–14)

III. The Family: A Force for Life

A. In the face of contrary human acts, the Christian family has a prophetic mission to witness to the primacy and preservation of life. (§15–17)

B. Marital chastity honors the sanctity of life and protects the dignity of human sexuality. (§16)

C. In deciding to give life to another person, spouses recognize God's stewardship given to them in this process; this is the ground for reverence in this process. (§19)

D. Responsible parenthood involves the properly formed conscience of Christian spouses, with God's direction through guidance of the Church. (§21)

IV. The Encyclical and Its Content

A. The theological framework for understanding the teaching in _Humanae Vitae_ lies in _Gaudium et Spes_. (§22–24)

B. Conjugal love encompasses a unified and procreative meaning. Each act must remain open to transmission of life. (§25–26)

C. _Humanae Vitae_ is a positive statement about conjugal love and responsible parenthood. (§28)

D. Natural methods of family regulation never involve a direct positive action against the possibility of human life. (§29–30)

E. The church's teaching, based on moral means to responsible parenthood, presupposes positive values. Prayerful discipline and use of natural methods can assist couples. (§32)

F. The ideal of chastity requires patient dedication. The objective morality and vision of this teaching need to be preached and lived. The church is called to patiently, steadfastly teach in this area. The sacrament of penance indicates the difficulty of these tasks. (§33–36)

V. The Encyclical and Conscience
A. Conscience is not a law unto itself. God's incarnate Word speaks and still enlightens in the Church of Christ. The role of conscience is a practical dictate, not a teacher of doctrine. (§37–38)

B. Conscience is the practical judgment by which we judge specific acts as good to be done or evil to be avoided. One is not to be forced to act contrary to one's conscience. (§39–40)

C. *Humanae Vitae* presents the authentic and authoritative teaching of the Church in this area. (§41)

D. Conscience should conform to divine law and the Church's teaching office, interpreting that law in light of the Gospel. (§42)

E. In the light of painful and difficult situations, the Church has responded with compassionate exhortation and clear teachings. Recourse to prayer and the sacraments is critical. (§43–44)

F. In the light of the objective evil of artificial contraception, married couples who have used artificial contraception are urged to use the sacrament of reconciliation to restore spiritual stability. (§45)

G. Negative reactions to the encyclical are explored.
   1. Many expected the Church to modify its teaching, yet the Church has maintained its consistent teaching. (§46–47)
   2. The authentic teaching of the Church calls for assent, even when the Pope is not speaking "ex cathedra."(§48)

VI. Norms of Licit Theological Dissent
A. Legitimate theological speculation and research can allow for licit dissent. Dissent with propriety is called for as the presumption is in favor of the Magisterium in non-infallible doctrine. (§49–53)

B. Leadership should support the Church's teaching on marriage without ambiguity. (§54)

VII. Family Spirituality

A. The bishops pledge support in the renewal of the family. (§55)

B. A sound spirituality of family life and prayer are encouraged. Theologians can assist in developing this vision. (§56–57)

C. Marriage preparation programs should be promoted in dioceses. (§58)

D. These efforts should include married couples and those who support *Humanae Vitae*. (§59)

VIII. The Education of Children in Sexuality Considered

A. The Church must support families in the education in sexuality of their children. (§60)

B. Parents are the primary educators in mutual consultation and shared responsibility. (§61)

C. Educators should be carefully selected for this task, and content of instruction should be age appropriate. (§62–63)

IX. The new American family is filled with tensions and needs.

A. The approach used by *Gaudium et Spes* provides an optimistic appraisal of the resilience and adaptability of the contemporary family, even in the midst of tremendous challenges. (§65–67)

B. Today's families focus on individualism and equalitarian role in marriage. (§68)

C. Modern media can strengthen family bonds. (§69)

D. Equality of men and women in society is being seen as a value. (§70)

E. Cultural changes create pressures. Communication skills in families needed. (§71)

F. Families have responsibility toward wider human family. (§72)

G. Wise social policy supports full family units and should be reflected in appropriate legislation and in implementation of public policy. (§73–74)

   1. Programs for food and housing should include the well being of the whole family. (§75–76)

   2. Families need income proportionate to their needs, and social policy should advocate for this. (§77–78)

3. Resources should be mobilized to assist families both nationally and globally in charity and justice. (§79)

4. Larger families, adoptive families, and foster families are commended. (§80–82)

H. Further threats to life are noted.

1. Society should be on the side of life and show reverence for life. (§83–84)

2. Procured abortion and infanticide are condemned. (§85–86)

X. Christian Optimism

A. The family is the school of deeper humanity. (§88)

B. Christian family is the image of God and sign of Church. (§89)

C. As the basic unit of human society, the family should be the object of civilization's concern.

D. Optimism is based on preserving the hope of married couples. (§91)

Key Quote

The prophetic mission of the family obliges it to fidelity to conjugal love in the face of the compromises and infidelities condoned in our culture. Its prophetic mission obliges the family to valiant hope in life, contradicting whatever forces seek to prevent, destroy, or impair life. In its emphasis on the virtues of fidelity and hope, so essential to the prophetic witness of the family, Christian sexual morality derives therefore, not from the inviolability of generative biology, but ultimately from the sanctity of life itself and the nobility of human sexuality. (§17)

Suggested Readings

Human Life in Our Day, in *Pastoral Letters of the U.S. Bishops* (vol. 3), 1962-1974, Hugh J. Nolan, ed. Washington, D.C.: Publications Office, NCCB/USCC, 1984, pp. 164-183.

Prieur, Michael R. *Married in the Lord* (rev.). Collegeville, MN: The Liturgical Press, 1978.

Also, see commentaries on *Humanae Vitae* in Carlen, Claudia, I.H.M., *The Papal Encyclicals* (vols. 1–5), pages 233-236.

Persona Humana

The Vatican Declaration on Certain Questions Regarding Sexual Ethics

Congregation for the Doctrine of the Faith

December 29, 1975

Major Areas of Concern
- Current issues
- Natural law
- Premarital sex
- Masturbation
- Homosexuality

As a result of dramatic world-wide changes in society, the pastoral application of the Church's teaching on sexuality was challenged. Topics being challenged included pre-marital sex, homosexuality, and masturbation. In response to questions posed to them, the Sacred Congregation for the Faith responded to specific inquires and concerns. This document confirms the use of natural law methodology as presented in *Humanae Vitae*. The objective basis for morality is reaffirmed.

I. The Present Situation
   A. The importance of sexuality as the principal trait of the human person is expressed.

B. Today's society glorifies sex.
1. Some people promote a licentious hedonism.
2. There is confusion about what Christians believe. (§1)

II. The Church cannot remain indifferent to this confusion.
A. The Sacred Congregation for the Doctrine of the Faith responds to inquiries on the topic. (§2)

III. Some basic principles are presented.
A. The essential order of our nature must be respected.

B. Sexuality is governed by immutable principles, which can be grasped by reason.

C. These principles are eternal, objective, and universal.
1. We must participate in this divine law. (§3)

IV. Morality is not an expression of a particular culture or of a certain moment in history.
A. Human nature is constant and the precepts of natural law have absolute value. (§4)

V. Sexual ethics concerns fundamental values of human life, and natural law applies.
A. Vatican Council II called for equal dignity of men and women while respecting their differences.

B. The Church's teaching comes from divine revelation and authentic interpretation of natural law.
1. The use of sexual function has its true meaning and morality only in marriage. (§5)

VI. The object of the present declaration is not to explain all abuses of sexual faculty, but to explain the Church's doctrine. (§6)

VII. Pre-marital sex is wrong even among those planning to marry.
A. Experience teaches that love must find its stability in marriage.
1. The conjugal contract is needed, especially because pre-marital relations usually exclude the possibility of children.
2. The Church holds that marriage consent must be sacramental. (§7)

VIII. Homosexuality

A. Homosexuality is opposed to the moral teaching of the Church and the Christian moral sense.

B. The sources of homosexuality can be transitory and curable, from bad example, habit, or lack of sexual development.

C. Homosexuality can be incurable because of constitution and must be treated with understanding. No pastoral method can give justification for homosexual activity.

D. Homosexuality is seen as intrinsically disordered. (§8)

IX. Masturbation is a grave moral disorder.

A. The deliberate use of the sexual faculty outside normal conjugal relations contradicts the finality of the faculty.

B. Sociological surveys are not a criterion of moral values.

C. Some reasons why this behavior continues are: innate weakness caused by original sin, loss of sense of God, commercialization of vice, licentiousness of entertainment, and neglect of modesty.

D. Judgments about masturbation should be based on the use of natural and supernatural means to avoid this temptation. (§9)

X. There is a tendency to minimize or deny the reality of grave sin.

A. Mortal sin is committed when:
   1. The action is in direct contempt of the love of God and neighbor.
   2. Something that is disordered is consciously and freely chosen for whatever reason.

B. The lessening of consent should be prudentially judged, yet it is false to assert that, in sexuality, mortal sins cannot be committed. (§10)

XI. Chastity is not a negative but rather a positive virtue. (§11)

A. It must be practiced according to mind of Christ. (Matthew 5:28)

B. Continence is a gift of the Holy Spirit. (Galatians 5:19–25; Ephesians 5:3–8)

C. It is a liberation from the passions. (Romans 6:7–8)

XII. True liberation does not suppress concupiscence. In order to lead a chaste life, the Church encourages:

A. discipline of the senses and mind, avoiding occasions of sin, observance of modesty, prayer, frequent reception of sacraments, accepting modesty and chastity. (§12)

XIII. **It is the obligation of bishops to instruct the faithful, provide sound doctrine in seminaries, and to make available catechetical instruction faithful to Christian doctrine. (§13)**

XIV. **Priests are obliged to alert the faithful to erroneous opinion and, as confessors, to enlighten persons' consciences. (§14)**

XV. **Parents are responsible for providing sex education suited to age and to form children's wills in accordance with Christian morals. (§15)**

XVI. **Those persons using social communications have an obligation to do so in accordance with Christian faith. (§16)**

XVII. **Young people have a right to moral values, and those who govern people or preside over educational settings must protect this right. (§17)**

Key Quote

Experience teaches us that love must find its safeguard in the stability of marriage if sexual intercourse is truly to respond to the requirements of its own finality, and to those of human dignity. These requirements call for a conjugal contract sanctioned and guaranteed by society—a contract which establishes a state of life of capital importance both for the exclusive union of the man and the woman and for the good of their family and of the human community. (§7)

Suggested Readings

May, William E. "The Vatican Declaration on Sexual Ethics and the Moral Methodology of Vatican II." *Linacre Quarterly.* May 1985, pp. 116-129.

Keane, Philip E., S.S. *Sexual Morality: A Catholic Perspective.* Paramus, NJ: Paulist Press, 1977.

[Latin Text: *Acta Apostolica Sedes* 68 (1968), 77-96]

Familiaris Consortio

On the Family
Pope John Paul II
December 15, 1981

Major Areas of Concern
- Family today
- Role of Christian family
- Forming community of persons
- Serving life
- Developing society
- Becoming Church
- Pastoral care of families

In this Apostolic Exhortation, Pope John Paul II summarizes the conclusions of the Synod on Families (1980). He highlights the role of support that the Church should provide to Christian married couples and their families. A vision of the Christian family is presented, and pastoral strategies to assist couples and families are suggested, especially for those populations (e.g., separated and divorced) experiencing some alienation from the Church.

John Paul II's personalistic language style is reflected in this document. *Familiaris Consortio* is a concrete response to specific concerns of couples and families (e.g., men and women's roles in society, birth control, divorce, engaged couples, faith and practice). The theological framework for the document reflects his prior writings and concerns. A covenant theology of marriage is expressed and the language of personalism replaces a natural law/canonical approach to the issues.

I. Introduction

A. The Church is at the service of the family. (§1)

B. The Synod of 1980 is in continuity with preceding Synods. (§2)

C. Marriage and family life is a precious value. (§3)

II. Bright Spots and Shadows for the Family Today

A. Today there is a need to understand the state of marriage and family. (§4)

B. Evangelical discernment is necessary. (§5)

C. The situation of the family in the world today is changing. (§6)

D. The influence of circumstances on the consciences of the faithful is recognized. (§7)

E. This era needs the Church's wisdom. (§8)

F. Gradualness and conversion are integral. (§9)

G. Inculturation must be recognized. (§10)

III. There is a plan of God for marriage and the family.

A. The person is the image of the God who is love. (§11)

B. Marriage is a reflection of the communion between God and people. (§12)

C. Jesus Christ, Bridegroom of the Church, mirrors the sacrament of matrimony. (§13)

D. Children are a precious gift of marriage. (§14)

E. The family is a communion of persons. (§15)

F. Marriage and virginity or celibacy are equal ways to show human and divine love. (§16)

IV. The Role of the Christian Family: "Family, become what you are!" (§17)

A. Forming a Community of Persons:

1. Love is the principle and power of communion. (§18)
2. The indivisible unity of conjugal communion is affirmed. (§19)
3. Marriage creates an indissoluble communion. (§20)
4. Marriage shapes the broader communion of the family, linking the natural with the supernatural. (§21)

5. Women's equality is expressed in the rights and role of women. (§22)
6. Women contribute to society through their work in the home and workplace. (§23)
7. Offenses against women's dignity need to be addressed directly. (§24)
8. Men should be challenged in their roles as husbands and fathers. (§25)
9. The rights of all children should be upheld. (§26)
10. Respect and care for the elderly in the family is essential. (§27)

B. Serving Life
  1. The transmission of life:
    a. Married couples are cooperators in the love of God the Creator. (§28)
    b. The Church's teaching and norm on the purposes of marriage are constant. (§29)
    c. The Church stands for life—rejecting contraception, sterilization, and abortion. (§30)
    d. A personalistic approach to this issue is needed. (§31)
    e. The unitive and procreative meanings of conjugal loving cannot be separated; Natural Family Planning is a tool to assist couples. (§32)
    f. The Church is a teacher for couples struggling with this. (§33)
    g. Couples should be supported in living out this ideal. (§34)
    h. The Church's role is to instill conviction and offer practical help. (§35)
  2. Education
    a. The right and duty of parents regarding education is paramount. (§36)
    b. The family educates the members in the essential values of human life. (§37)
    c. The mission to educate is directly linked to the sacrament of marriage. (§38)
    d. The first experience of the Church occurs through family life. (§39)
    e. The family agrees to work collaboratively with others in education of children. (§40)
    f. Married couples serve life by caring for others, e.g., adoption and foster care. (§41)

C. Participating in the Development of Society
   1. The family is the first and most vital cell of society. (§42)
   2. Family life is an experience of communion and sharing. (§43)
   3. Families should be actively involved in social and political concerns. (§44)
   4. Society should be at the service of the family. (§45)
   5. The Charter of Family Rights is spelled out. (§46) (See pp. 64–66 of this volume for document.)
   6. The Christian family should show a preferential option for the poor and disadvantaged. (§47)
   7. The family must work for a new international order. (§48)

D. Sharing in the Life and Mission of the Church
   1. The family exists within the Church's proclamation of the Word and sacraments. (§49)
   2. The family must be at the service of Church and society. (§50)
      a. The Christian family should be a believing and evangelizing community.
         i. Faith as the discovery and admiring awareness of God's plan for the family: faith is strengthened through the experience of marriage and family. (§51)
         ii. The Christian family participates in the ministry of evangelism. (§52)
         iii. Ecclesial service: One's daily life is where the Gospel is proclaimed. (§53)
         iv. Living the Gospel as family is a form of missionary activity. (§54)
      b. The Christian family as a community in dialogue with God.
         i. Daily family life expresses a means of holiness. (§55)
         ii. The grace of the sacrament of marriage is an ongoing support to couples and families. (§56)
         iii. Marriages can be strengthened through reception of the Eucharist. (§57)
         iv. The sacrament of conversion and reconciliation are additional tools of support. (§58)
         v. Family prayer draws all closer to God and to each other. (§59)
         vi. Married couples are educators in prayer. (§60)
         vii. Liturgical prayer and private prayer are vital tools for spiritual growth. (§61)
         viii. Prayer is linked to the Christian life and family. (§62)

   c. The Christian family as a community at the service of hu-
      manity.
      i. Marriage can be a way to express the new commandment
         of love. (§63)
      ii. Families are called to discover the image of God in each
          brother and sister. (§64)

V. Pastoral Care of the Family: Stages, Structures, Agents, and Situations

   A. Stages of Pastoral Care of the Family
      1. The Church journeys with the Christian family through life.
         (§65)
      2. Preparation for marriage should occur over the years. (§66)
      3. The celebration of marriage ought to reflect thorough prepara-
         tion. (§67)
      4. The Church should challenge engaged couples who are weak
         in faith and practice. (§68)
      5. The Church should foster pastoral care after marriage. (§69)

   B. Structures of Family Pastoral Care
      1. The global and local Church needs to support families. (§70)
      2. The family should care for those most in need. (§71)
      3. Solidarity between families is reflected in the Gospel vision.
         (§72)
      4. Bishops and priests should support families in teaching and
         education. (§73)
      5. Men and women religious provide active care for couples and
         families. (§74)
      6. Lay specialists contribute their expertise to promoting family
         life. (§75)
      7. The media is challenged to provide family values. (§76)

   C. Agents of the Pastoral Care of the Family
      1. Specific needs of families can be responded to by service. (§77)
      2. Mixed marriages are acknowledged and support encouraged.
         (§78)
      3. Couples not married according to church law should be en-
         couraged and assisted to regularize their union. These in-
         clude:
         a. Trial marriages
         b. De facto free unions

    c. Catholics in civil marriages

    d. Separated or divorced persons who have not remarried should be supported.

    e. Divorced persons who have remarried are encouraged to rectify their situation. (§79)

  4. Those without a family should be welcomed into families. (§80)

  5. Conclusion: "The future of humanity passes by way of the family." (§81)

Key Quote

The family, which is founded and given by love, is a community of persons: of husband and wife, of parents and children, of relatives. Its first task is to live with fidelity the reality of communion in a constant effort to develop an authentic community of persons.

The inner principle of that task, its permanent power and its final goal is love: Without love the family is not a community of persons and, in the same way, without love the family cannot live, grow, and perfect itself as an authentic community of persons…. "Man cannot live without love. He remains a being that is incomprehensible for himself, his life is senseless, if love is not revealed to him, if he does not encounter love, if he does not experience it and make it his own, if he does not participate intimately in it." (§18)

Suggested Readings

A Positive Vision for Family Life—A Resource Guide for Pope John Paul II's Apostolic Exhortation Familiaris Consortio. Ed. by Rev Thomas Lynch and Valerie Dillon. Commission on Marriage and Family Life. Department of Education, USCC, 1985.

Hogan, Richard M., and LeVoir, John M. *Covenant of Love: Pope John Paul II on Sexuality, Marriage, and Family in the Modern World.* (reprint) San Francisco: Ignatius Press, 1986.

Saxton, Stanley L., et al. *The Changing Family: Views from Theology and the Social Sciences in the Light of the Apostolic Exhortation Familaris Consortio.* Chicago: Loyola University Press, 1984.

The Charter of the Rights of the Family

Statement Presented by the Holy See
October 22, 1983

Major Areas of Concern
- Rights of individuals
- Rights of family
- Duties of family

This document reflects the rights and duties of families in society and, conversely, the rights and duties of society toward the family. It suggests "a blueprint for building a healthy, human society founded on the integrity of family life." It is intended to express a theoretical basis for understanding the family and is addressed mainly to governments. Modeled upon the United Nations' Charter of Human Rights, a preliminary version of this document is found in §46 of *Familiaris Consortio*.

The Charter came about as a result of a request made by the Synod of Bishops in 1980. It develops a natural law explanation of the rights proposed and represents a process of thought already present in other church documents.

I. Preamble
    A. The rights of the person have a social base—grounded in the family.

B. The family is based on marriage—freely chosen and open to new life.

C. The family teaches and conveys "cultural, educational, social, spiritual, and religious values."

D. The family's wisdom comes through a multigenerational process.

E. On all levels, society must protect the family.

F. The church has as its mission to provide and safeguard families.

II. Charter of the Rights of the Family

A. There is a natural right to choose one's status in life. Marriage and the establishment of a family is a freely chosen right to be safeguarded by society.

B. Spouses should not be coerced into marriage. It should be freely chosen, with religious freedom safeguarding this right. (§2)

C. Couples have the right to found a family, including the number and spacing of children within the objective moral order. No government has the right to restrict this. Society or governments cannot impose abortion, birth control, or sterilization. (§3)

D. Human life has dignity from conception on. All children should be protected and nurtured, especially orphans, foster children, adopted children, and handicapped children. (§4)

E. Parents are primary educators of their children and have a right to freely choose their child's education in line with their beliefs. Society and governments cannot regulate this. (§5)

F. Families in society should mutually assist one another in their process. (§6)

G. Religious freedom for families should be safeguarded. (§7)

H. The family should be involved in social and political processes of society. Government should promote the good and represent the interests of families. (§8)

I. Family policy of governments should respond for the social welfare of families, especially the disenfranchised (unemployed, poor, elderly, physically or mentally handicapped). (§9)

J. Work in society should be ordered so that family values can be supported. A "family wage" is supported. (§10)

K. Adequate housing should be made accessible to families. (§11)

L. Migrant and immigrant family needs should be supported. (§12)

Key Quote
The family constitutes, much more than a juridical, social, and economic unit, a community of love and solidarity which is uniquely suited to teach and transmit cultural, ethical, social, spiritual, and religious values, essential for the development and well being of its own members and of society. (Preamble-E)

Suggested Readings
McCormick, Richard, S.J. "Family Rights and Public Policy" in *In All Things: Religious Faith and American Culture.* Robert J. Daly, S.J., ed. Kansas City: Sheed & Ward, 1990.

Charter of the Rights of the Family (Vatican City: Vatican Polyglot Press, October 22, 1983).

Codex Iuris Canonici

The Code of Canon Law
Pope John Paul II
January 25, 1983

Major Areas of Concern

- Nature of Marriage: General Principles (cc. 1055–1062)
- Preliminaries to Marriage (cc. 1063–1072)
- Impediments and Their Dispensation (cc. 1073–1082)
- Diriment Impediments (cc. 1083–1094)
- Matrimonial Consent (cc. 1095–1107)
- The Form of Marriage (cc. 1108–1123)
- Mixed Marriages (cc. 1124–1129)
- Secret Marriages (cc. 1130–1133)
- Consequences of Marriage (cc. 1134-1140)
- Separation, Annulment, and Remarriage (cc. 1141–1155)
- Convalidation and Sanation of Marriage (cc. 1156–1165)

The revised Code of Canon Law, promulgated on January 25, 1983, was the culmination of twenty years of consultation within the Church. The code, the official law of the Catholic Church, expresses our theology and tradition in legal form. Of the 1754 Canons, 111 are focused on marriage (cc. 1055–1165). Divided into ten chapters, the code's treatment of marriage includes a wide range of topics. Noteworthy is the use of Vatican II's concept of covenant from *Gaudium et Spes*'s treatment of marriage. Advances in the new code are: a firmer theological grounding of this covenant theme, recognition of the impact of modern psychology and psychiatry, decentralization of the law, and ecumenical advances. A significant development was that "consent" could be nullified if a person suffered from a serious psychological disorder that prevented him or her from assuming the obligations of marriage.

The code has been called the "final document of Vatican II" because of the influence of the council on its revision. In his promulgation of the code, John Paul II suggested that the richness of the council's doctrine was translated into canonical language in this revision. The First Synod of Bishops approved the ten principles for the revision of the code. The revision of the code began shortly after Vatican II, and in 1981 the final document was sent to the Pope for his review and proclamation.

In the revision of the section on marriage, the influence of the council constitution *Gaudium et Spes* is evident. A personalist approach is given to the purposes of marriage. The canons speak first of the essence of marriage and then of its purpose. Within the code, "rotal jurisprudence," which had been developed since Vatican II, has been sanctioned.

I. Introduction

    A. Marriage between husband and wife is a covenant and partnership.

       1. This covenant is ordered to the good of the spouses and the procreation and education of children. (c. 1055)

       2. Essential properties of marriage are unity and indissolubility. (c. 1056)

       3. Through the consent of the will, man and woman enter into an irrevocable covenant. (c. 1057)

       4. Those not prohibited by law are free to marry. (c. 1058)

       5. Civil authority has the right to create law over the civil aspects of marriage. (c. 1059)

       6. All marriages are presumed to be valid, and are ratified, and when sexual intercourse has occurred they are then "ratified and consummated" and cannot be dissolved. (cc. 1060, 1061, 1141)

II. Pastoral care and marriage preparation are the responsibility of the whole Christian community. (c. 1063)

    A. Bishops are responsible for organizing this effort. (c. 1065)

    B. Couples preparing for matrimony should have received the sacrament of confirmation and are encouraged to receive penance and the Eucharist. (c. 1065)

C. No impediments should block sacramental marriage. (cc. 1066, 1069–1070)

    1. Problematic couples, especially young people, need attention in this preparation process. (cc. 1070, 1072)

III. Impediments and their Dispensation/Diriment Impediments are presented. (c. 1073)

A. Impediments to valid exchange of consent are simplified.

    1. Twelve impediments are noted. They are: age, impotence, prior bond, disparity of cult, orders, vows of chastity, abduction, conjugicide, consanguinity, affinity, public propriety, adoption. (cc. 1083–1094)

    2. Diocesan bishop, and those he has delegated to do so, can grant dispensations. (cc. 1078–1080)

    3. Dispensations from holy orders, vows of chastity, and conjugicide are reserved to the Holy See. (c. 1078)

IV. Matrimonial consent occurs in the giving and accepting of each other in order to establish marriage. (c. 1057)

A. Couples must be present together for this exchange of consent (c. 1104) and the internal consent is presumed to coincide with the words spoken. (c.1101.1)

V. Eight possible defects of marital consent are possible:

A. Incapacity (c. 1095); ignorance (c. 1196); error about person (c. 1097); fraud (c. 1098); error about marriage (c. 1099); simulation (c. 1101.2); condition (c. 1102); force or fear (c. 1103).

VI. The canonical form for marriage includes:

A. Either the presence of the local pastor or bishop and two witnesses, or it can be delegated to a deacon, or in exceptional circumstances, another person. (cc. 1108–1123)

VII. Mixed marriages are given support and are not strictly forbidden. Only the Catholic partner is asked to promise to do his or her best to see that the children will be baptized in the Catholic Church and educated in the same religion. (cc. 1124–1129)

VIII. Secret marriages must follow from grave cause and all are

bound to the obligation of secrecy. Canonical norms must be followed. (cc. 1131–1133)

IX. **With valid sacramental marriage a perpetual and exclusive bond is created. (c. 1134)**
   A. Spouses have equal obligations and rights pertaining to the partnership of conjugal life. (c. 1135)

   B. Parents have duty and primary right to do all in their power to see to the physical, social, cultural, moral, and religious upbringing of their children. (c. 1136)

X. **The basis for the separation of spouses is presented.**
   A. Dissolution of the bond can occur only:
      1. If it was not consummated, or if it is a non-sacramental marriage that is either a union between two baptized persons or between a baptized and a non-baptized person.
      2. Pauline privilege is still present. (cc. 1141–1150)

   B. Separation is permitted when injury or substantial hurt is evidenced. (cc. 1151–1155)

   C. Invalid marriages can be rendered valid when necessary dispensation is given, missing formalities supplied, or by granting the consent that was withheld. (cc. 1156–1165)

Key Quote

The matrimonial covenant by which a man and a woman establish between themselves a partnership of the whole of life, is by its nature ordered toward the good of the spouses and the procreation and education of offspring; this covenant between baptized persons had been raised by Christ the Lord to the dignity of a sacrament. (Canon 1055 §1)

For this reason, a matrimonial contract cannot validly exist between baptized persons unless it is also a sacrament by that fact. (Canon 1055 §2)

Suggested Readings

Code of Canon Law: Latin-English Edition. Washington, D.C.: Canon Law Society of America, 1983.

Code of Canons of the Eastern Church: Latin-English Edition. Washington, D.C.: Canon Law Society of America, 1990.

Coriden, James A. *An Introduction to Canon Law*. Mahwah, NJ: Paulist Press, 1991.

Coriden, James A., et al. *The Code of Canon Law: A Text and Commentary*. Mahwah, NJ: Paulist Press, 1985.

Pastoral Care of the Homosexual Person

Congregation for the Doctrine of the Faith
October 1, 1986

Major Areas of Concern
- Dignity of the homosexual person
- Scripture, tradition support pastoral practice

This document responds to requests from some conferences of bishops concerned about distortions of Church teaching on the topic of homosexuality and about pastoral practice to the homosexual population. The Congregation for the Doctrine of the Faith, noting the increased public debate in society and the Church on the topic of homosexuality, and further noting that some of the positions being taken in this debate were contrary to the Church's teaching, chose to respond through this document. It positively affirms that the inclination toward homosexuality is not a sin and that the human dignity of the person should be recognized. Pastoral practice consistent with Church teaching is affirmed.

I. The issue of homosexuality and the evaluation of homosexual acts are debated today. (¶1)

II. Catholic moral viewpoint is based on human reason illumined by faith.

A. Science is helpful but needs to go beyond.

B. The Church has the responsibility to provide pastoral care.

C. This care based on study, active concern, and honest theologically well-based counsel. (¶2)

III. Prior documentation (*Persona Humana*, see p. 54) notes distinction between homosexual condition or tendency, and individual homosexual actions.

A. The teaching of the Church is reaffirmed with clarification. The particular inclination is not sin, but is "more ordered toward an intrinsic moral evil."

B. Inclination seen as an objective disorder.

C. Homosexual activity is not a morally acceptable option. (¶3)

IV. Scripture and Tradition of the Church are reaffirmed.

A. Scriptural interpretation should be in accord with Tradition. (¶4)

B. Theology of creation in Genesis sees complementarity of sexes as reflecting unity of Creator. (¶5)

C. Old and New Testament passages on topic support teaching. Contemporary exegesis distorts tradition. (¶6)

D. In marital relationship sexual expression morally good.

E. Engaging in homosexual acts is immoral.

F. Homosexual activity lacks complementarity and ability to transmit life. (¶7)

G. Church teaching consistent with Scriptural perspective.

H. Materialism denies transcendent nature of person. (¶8)

V. The Church should not respond to pressure for change in teaching or pastoral practice.

A. The Church cannot give in to pressure groups. (¶9)

B. The Church rejects violence, prejudice, and discrimination.

C. The dignity of the person should be upheld in action and laws. (¶10)

VI. The assumptions that all homosexual behavior is compulsive are false. (¶11)

A. Homosexuals should embrace will of God in their lives.

B. A celibate life style for Christian homosexuals is called for. (¶12)

VII. The Church calls for clear teaching and pastoral ministry. (¶13)

A. The Church cannot endorse programs and groups that go contrary to Magisterium, yet should provide supportive initiatives. (¶14)

B. Programs should include spiritual components—prayer, sacraments, and counseling. (¶15)

VIII. Fundamental identity of person goes beyond sexual orientation. (¶16)

IX. The Bishops are asked to provide special care in determining pastoral ministers in this area.

A. Catechetical programs should reflect truth about human sexuality.

B. Support—including use of church facilities—should be revoked from groups not clearly presenting teaching of the Church. (¶17)

X. The Church is called to minister to all who suffer. (¶18)

Key Quote

What, then, are homosexual persons to do who seek to follow the Lord? Fundamentally, they are called to reenact the will of God in their life by joining whatever sufferings and difficulties they experience in virtue of their condition to the sacrifice of the Lord's cross. That cross, for the believer, is a fruitful sacrifice since from that death comes life and redemption. While any call to carry the cross or to understand a Christian's suffering in this way will predictably be met with bitter ridicule by some, it should be remembered that this is the way to eternal life for *all* who follow Christ. (¶12)

Suggested Readings

Harvey, John, O.S.F.S. *The Homosexual Person—New Thinking in Pastoral Care.* Ignatius Press: San Francisco, 1987.

Williams, Bruce, O.P. "Homosexuality: The New Vatican Statement," in *Theological Studies* 48 (1987), pp. 259-277.

Donum Vitae

*Instruction on Respect for Human Life
and the Dignity of Procreation*

Congregation for the Doctrine of the Faith

February 22, 1987

Major Areas of Concern
- Personhood
- Procreation in conjugal act
- Heterologous artificial fertilization
- Homologous artificial fertilization
- Church's concern for infertile couples

This instruction, a response to new scientific and technological developments, focuses on the origin of human persons. The final criteria for procreation cannot be based solely on science. Life is a gift, and we as human persons should not manipulate this collaborative creative process. Heterologous artificial fertilization and homologous artificial fertilization are morally objectionable. Concidentally, the document was published at the time of the "Baby M" case in New Jersey in 1987. *The New York Times* (March 11, 1987) printed the entire document. The Church sought to provide moral guidance and direction to Catholic physicians, hospitals, and the broader community during the time of rapid growth in "reproductive technologies." The Gamete Intrafallopi-

---

an Transfer (GIFT) and Tubule Ovum Transfer with Sperm (TOTS) are two methods seen as morally acceptable.

(Though this point may seem subtle, it is critical: The origin of human personhood resides within the will of God. The married couple, in an act of cooperation with the Creator, brings forth a human life. Though the couple anticipates the birth of this new life, it is God alone who knows who that child is.)

I. Foreword

Purpose of document: to respond to questions about interventions in the beginnings of human life.

Structure of document:
- introduction
- first part—respect for human embryos
- second part—interventions upon human procreation
- third part—moral teachings and law.

II. Introduction

A. Biomedical Research and the Teaching of the Church
1. Life is a gift. The Church presents the criterion of moral judgments in relation to human life and its beginnings. (¶1–5)

B. Science and technology are at the service of the human person, assisting the conscience that guides us according to the will of God. (¶6–8)

C. Anthropology and Procedures in the Biomedical Field
1. The human person is a "unified totality" of body and soul. (¶9–10)
2. Natural moral law gives us purpose, rights, and duties. (¶11)
3. The use of medical and the biological sciences must be read in the light of the dignity of the human person. (¶12–14)

D. Fundamental criteria for a moral judgment is twofold:
1. Human life is inviolable from the moment of conception to the last moment of life. (¶15–16)
2. The transmission of human life in marriage is inviolable. (¶17–18)

E. Teachings of the Magisterium
1. Human life is sacred because of "the creative action of God." (¶19–20)

2. Authentic human procreation can occur only within marriage. (¶21)

3. [transitional segment (¶22)]

III. Human procreation calls for the collaboration of spouses with God.

A. Respect for Human Embryos

1. What respect is due to the human embryo, taking into account his nature and identity? (¶23)

   a. From the moment of fertilization, the new life is a human being with unconditional respect and moral rights. (¶24–27)

   b. Because the embryo must be treated as a person, it needs to be cared for as any other human being. (¶28)

2. Is prenatal diagnosis morally licit?

   a. For purposes of diagnosis it is morally licit, but for use to determine abortion, morally illicit. (¶31–32)

3. Are therapeutic procedures carried out on the human embryo licit?

   a. These are morally acceptable, assuming free and informed consent, for healing of maladies (e.g., chromosomal defects). (¶33–35)

4. How is one to evaluate, morally, research and experimentation on human embryos and fetuses?

   a. Research operations upon live embryos are morally unacceptable. These embryos suffer experimental manipulation and exploitation. (¶36–42)

5. How is one to evaluate, morally, the use for research purposes of embryos obtained by fertilization "in vitro"?

   a. "In vitro" procedures that result in the embryo being destroyed are morally unacceptable and are illicit when damage or possible grave risks to the embryo are present. (¶42–45)

6. What judgment should be made on other procedures of manipulating embryos connected with the "techniques of human reproduction"?

   a. Cloning and parthenogenesis are contrary to moral law. (¶46–47)

   b. Selecting human beings according to sex or other characteristics is against personal dignity. (¶48)

IV. Interventions Upon Human Procreation

A. Fertilization of an ovum in a test tube ("in vitro" fertilization) and artificial insemination through transfer into the woman's genital tract of previously collected sperm are reviewed. (¶49–50)

B. Some "spare" embryos are destroyed in these procedures. (¶51–54)

C. Heterologous Artificial Fertilization [at least one donor other than the married couple]
1. Responsible procreation is the fruit of marriage. (¶55–58)
2. The rights of the child include conception in the womb, to be brought into the world, and raised in marriage. (¶59)
3. This method of fertilization is contrary to the unity of marriage and dignity of procreation of the human person. (¶61–65)
4. Surrogate motherhood is morally illicit. It is contrary to the unity of marriage and the dignity of procreation of the human person. (¶66–67)
5. [transitional segment (¶68)]

D. Homologous Artificial Fertilization ["in vitro" fertilization, embryo transfer and artificial insemination between husband and wife—technique using gametes of the married couple.]
1. Unitive and procreative functions are inseparable. Homologous artificial fertilization separates the goods and meaning of marriage. (¶69–72)
2. Humans have unity of body and spirit, which are separated in homologous insemination. (¶73–75)
3. Conception should occur through the conjugal act. (¶76)
4. "In vitro" conception does not flow from a specific act of conjugal communion. (¶77)
5. The IVF process cannot use the logic of a desire for a child as the basis of moral evaluation. (¶78)
   a. IVF can lead to the destruction of human embryos and is thus morally unacceptable. (¶79)
   b. The use of technology for IVF demeans the dignity of both parents and children. (¶80)
   c. IVF conception is not the result and fruit of a conjugal act. Thus it violates the divine plan. (¶81)
   d. Homologous IVF and Embryo Transplants violate the dignity of procreation and of conjugal union. (¶82–84)

E. Homologous insemination, if it facilitates a conjugal act, can be morally acceptable. (GIFT and TOTS: artificial insemination through the use of masturbation is morally unacceptable.) (¶85)

F. Medical intervention can assist but not substitute for the conjugal act. The physical expression of the bond of love between spouses cannot be replaced by medical technology. (¶89)

G. Couples suffering sterility should seek other means (adoption, foster care) to share their life and love. (¶91–96)

V. Moral and Civil Law

A. Civil law should protect the right to life from the moment of conception until death. (¶97–99)

B. The rights of marriage and family and especially conception should be upheld. (¶100)

C. The civil law should respect and protect the unborn child. (¶101–102)

D. Political authority must be at the service of the people. (¶103)

E. Legislation should prohibit embryo banks, post-mortem insemination, and "surrogate motherhood." (¶104)

F. Civil law should conform to the fundamental norms of moral law. (¶105–107)

VI. Conclusion

A. The Congregation for Doctrine of Faith encourages support of the Magisterium's teaching on this matter. (¶108–112)

Key Quote

It would, on the one hand, be illusory to claim that scientific research and its applications are morally neutral; on the other hand, one cannot derive criteria for guidance from mere technical efficiency, from research's possible usefulness to some at the expense of others, or, worse still, from prevailing ideologies. Thus science and technology require, for their own intrinsic meaning, an unconditional respect for the fundamental criteria of the moral law; that is to say, they must be at the service of the human person, of his inalienable rights and his true and integral good according to the design and will of God. (¶7)

The rapid development of technological discoveries gives greater urgency to this need to respect the criteria just mentioned; science without conscience can only lead to man's ruin. "Our era needs such wisdom more than bygone ages if the discoveries made by man are to be further humanized. For the future of the world stands in peril unless wiser people are forthcoming." (¶8)

Suggested Readings

Albacete, Lorenzo M. *Commentary on Instruction on Respect for Human Life in its Origin and on the Dignity of Procreation*. Boston: St. Paul Editions, 1987.

Mulligan, James J. *Choose Life*. Braintree, MA: The Pope John Center, 1991. [Numbering used for this document is taken from the text above.]

Shannon, Thomas A., and Lisa Sowle Cahill. *Religion and Artificial Reproduction: An Inquiry into the Vatican "Instruction on Respect for Human Life in Its Origin and on the Dignity of the Human Person."* New York: Crossroad Publishing Company, 1988.

Mulieris Dignitatem

On the Dignity and Vocation of Women
Pope John Paul II
August 15, 1988

Major Areas of Concern
- Dignity of person
- Vocation
- Women
- Mary as model

The Synod of Bishops in 1987, studying the vocation and mission of the laity, recommended a further study of the anthropological and theological basis needed to address the problems connected with the meaning and dignity of being a woman and being a man. Here John Paul II uses his phenomenological system to generate a reflection on the nature and dignity of woman using both Scripture and tradition. He affirms the inherent dignity and equality of women and men, with the role of Mary exemplifying the response of all humans to God. The text is written in the style of a meditation.

I. Introduction
    A. Woman's dignity stands at the critical point of divine revelation. (§1)

---

    1. Mary's union with God exceeds all prior human expectation (§2–3)

  B. The revelation of the fullness of time confirms the extraordinary dignity of (the) woman as the exemplar of humanity in union with God. Mary's motherhood embraces the whole person, not merely the body. (§4)

    1. Mary takes her place as a woman within the messianic service of Christ. This is the basis for reflection on the dignity and vocation of women.

    2. No human being, male or female, can attain human fulfillment apart from the image and likeness of God. (§5)

II. Humankind is the image and likeness of God.

  A. Humankind is the high point of creation in the visible world. Both genders are equal in their humanity (cf. Genesis 1:27).

  B. Humankind is a rational being, and so male and female are able to dominate other creatures in the world. (§6)

  C. Within the biblical account of the creation of man and woman is the institution of marriage. Here one's masculinity and femininity is fully revealed. (§7)

  D. Revelation takes place through divine activity within the limits of human ability. (§8)

III. Eve and Mary stand in contrast as women of faith.

  A. The mystery of evil and sin emphasize the break in the original unity between God and God's creatures. Sin diminishes human nature. It erodes the image and likeness of God. (§9)

  B. The disturbance of the original relationship between man and woman corresponds to their individual dignity as human persons.

    1. Women cannot become objects for men and likewise men for women.

      a. The personal resources of femininity are in no way inferior to masculinity. There is no need for women to take upon themselves contradictory male traits. (§10)

      b. Mary is the foundation of the new order of creation in Christ. She is the first and most blessed among women. (§11)

IV. Jesus Christ proclaimed the true dignity of women and their vocation against the culture of his time. (§12)

A. Jesus' words and works express the true respect and honor due to women. (§13)

B. The historical situation of women oppressed by male injustice is clearly made in Jesus' statements about adultery. Man is called to see woman as equal in dignity (cf. John 8:3–11 and Matthew 5:28). (§14)

C. The women of the Gospels, liberated by its truth, are models of discipleship for the Church in every age. (§15)

D. Women are the first to bear witness to the Resurrection. They are equally capable of embracing and proclaiming the Gospel. (§16)

E. Through virginity and motherhood, women fulfill their humanity. Mary, mother of God, is the foremost model. (§17)
   1. Motherhood, joined to the mutual gift of self giving in marriage, is linked to the nature of being woman. The woman's distinct role in the creation of new life is distinct from the male's contribution in this process. (§18)
   2. The woman has priority over man in education of children because of her unique relationship with the child. Women nurture all humankind because of their motherhood. Mary exemplifies this fully. (§19)
   3. Celibacy for the sake of the Kingdom is inseparable from Jesus and his radical proclamation of the Reign of God. (§20)
   4. Spousal love is unitive and procreative, both in married life and celibacy, corresponding to the truth of the human person. (§21)
   5. The Church, by analogy, is both mother and virgin. (§22)

F. The Church is the Bride of Christ.
   1. Ephesians 5:25–32 is significant because it encapsulates the scriptural image of spousal love in Christ, who is the Bridegroom wedded to his Church, the Bride. (§23)
   2. In a husband's love of his wife, there is a fundamental affirmation of the woman as a person.
   3. There is a need for mutual subjection out of reverence for Christ. (§24)
   4. Since all human beings are called through the Church to be the Bride of Christ, the "feminine" element becomes a symbol for all that is human. (§25)

    5. Christ's linking the Eucharist to priestly apostolic service pre-cludes women in this character. (§26)

    6. Throughout history of church women play an active and sig-nificant role in the life of the Church. (§27)

G. In the face of change, a return to the original understanding of vo-cation of woman is vital. (§28)

    1. Woman was called into creation as man's helper; the dignity of woman is held in highest order. (§29)

    2. Woman can truly find herself in the giving of love to another. (§30)

    3. Within the women of every age "the great works of God" are accomplished. The Church gives thanks for each and every woman. She calls for an appreciation of the gifts of the Spirit among women. (§31)

Key Quote

...the Church gives thanks for each and every woman...they as-sume, together with men, a common responsibility for the des-tiny of humanity...The Church gives thanks for all the manifes-tations of the feminine "genius" which have appeared in the course of history, in the midst of all peoples and nations...she gives thanks for all the fruits of feminine holiness. The Church asks at the same time that these invaluable "manifestations of the Spirit" (cf. 1 Corinthians 12:4ff.),...may be attentively recog-nized and appreciated so that they may return for the common good of the Church and for humanity, especially in our times. (§31)

Suggested Readings

Butler, Sara. "The Priest as Sacrament of Christ, the Bridegroom" *Worship* (November 1992), 408-417.

One in Christ Jesus—Toward a Pastoral Response to the Concerns of Women for Church and Society. (Ad Hoc Committee for Pastoral Response to Women's Concerns, NCCB, November 1992) Washington, D.C.: Of-fice of Publishing Services, USCC.

Christifideles Laici

*On the Vocation and Mission
of the Lay Faithful*
Pope John Paul II
December 30, 1988

Major Areas of Concern
- Dignity of the human person
- Critical role of the Christian family in society

This exhortation was the result of the 1987 Synod of Bishops and derives its support from the parable of the laborers in the vineyard (Matthew 20:1–2). It places the responsibility for the advancement of the Gospel in the present age upon all of the Christian faithful, noting the particular tasks to which the lay faithful are especially suited. The document is intended to be a faithful expression of the findings of the synod. It is also intended to stir and foster a profound awareness among all the faithful of that responsibility shared as a group and as individuals in the communion and mission of the Church. (§1–2)

I. The Dignity of the Human Person is the foundation.

A. The sacredness of the human person cannot be violated as it is established by God.

---

1. Fundamental rights do exist and have been violated. These rights include the rights to housing and work, to a family and responsible parenthood. (§5)
2. Through faith and baptism, members of the Church are incorporated into the body of Christ. The image of that communion is referred to by Christ himself in the image of the vine and branches (John 15:5). (§11–12)

II. The Family is the origin of the duty to society.

A. The family is the basic cell of society in which the duty of the lay faithful emerges.
   1. Within the family the work of the lay faithful is to promote that family.
   2. As whole civilizations depend upon the family for their development, the formation of the Christian family assumes its proper role.

B. The Charter of Rights of the Family specifies a working program for the lay faithful. (§40)

Key Quote

The lay faithful's duty to society primarily begins in marriage and in the family. This duty can only be fulfilled adequately with the conviction of the unique and irreplaceable value that the family has in the development of society and the Church herself.

The family is the basic cell of society. It is the cradle of life and love, the place in which the individual "is born" and "grows." Therefore, a primary concern is reserved for this community, especially in those times when human egoism, the anti-birth campaign, totalitarian politics, situations of poverty, material, cultural, and moral misery, threaten to make these very springs of life dry up. (§40)

Suggested Reading

Doohan, Leonard. *John Paul II and the Laity.* Le Jacq Publishing, Inc., 1984.

[Latin text: *Acta Apostolica Sedes*, 61 (1989), 393-521]

Ordo Celebrandi Matrimonium

The Order of Celebrating Marriage,
Second Edition

Congregation for Divine Worship and the Discipline
of the Sacraments

March 19, 1990

The reforms of the second Vatican Council have touched all aspects of Church life. The most apparent changes occurred within the liturgy. Sacramental and devotional rites were remodeled in the light of pastoral and theological directions that emerged from the council. Changes in the Order of Celebrating Marriage reflect the understanding of the Vatican Council and the era that followed. The care given to the reform of this rite can be seen in its focus on the formation of a Christian couple, by the grace of God, into a Christian family. The inclusion of an explicit invocation of the Holy Spirit (*epiclesis*) within the nuptial blessings parallels the reform in the ordination rites for priests and deacons. Additionally, these blessings are more inclusive of the groom than were the first revision of the marriage rites.

I. Introduction—On the Importance and Dignity of the Sacrament of Marriage

II. Recent church teachings on the sacrament of marriage are noted. (¶1–11)

III. **Preparing engaged couples is the responsibility of the entire church community including the bishop, the parish priests, and the laity. (¶12)**

   A. Local norms and guidelines (national conferences of bishops, dioceses) should assist in this pastoral care. (¶13)

   B. Local pastors assist through their preaching, personal preparation of the engaged, the effective liturgical celebration, and continued support of married couples. (¶14)

   C. An adequate preparation time is needed. (¶15)

   D. Faith is presupposed in the preparation. A catechesis in marriage and family should be provided. (¶16–17)

   E. The sacraments of initiation should be completed. (¶18)

   F. No impediments are allowable. (¶19)

   G. This preparation time can be an occasion for evangelization. (¶20)

   H. When a couple rejects the Church and its teaching, that couple cannot enter the sacrament of matrimony. (¶21)

   I. Special cases (e.g., marriage to an unbaptized party) must be reviewed carefully. (¶22)

   J. The priest celebrating the Mass and receiving the vows should ordinarily prepare the engaged couple. (¶23)

   K. Deacons may preside at the celebration of the sacrament when provided with the appropriate faculties. (¶24)

   L. With the proper faculties, delegated lay persons may prepare the couple and receive the consent of the spouses. (¶25)

   M. The entire Christian community should cooperate especially in the proximate preparation. (¶26)

   N. Marriages can be celebrated in the parish of either spouse or at another site with proper permission. (¶27)

IV. **The Celebration of Marriage**

   A. Preparation

   1. Celebrations should occur within the parish community. They can be celebrated during the Sunday assembly. (¶28)

   2. The celebration can occur during the Mass or in a ceremony. (¶29)

3. The music should express the faith of the church and be appropriate. (¶30)
4. The wedding liturgy must reflect the liturgical season. (¶32)

B. The Rite to be Used
1. Specific directives for the celebration of marriage within the Mass and outside of the Mass are noted. (¶33–38)
   a. In marriages between a Catholic and baptized non-Catholic the rite of marriage outside of Mass is to be used.

V. Adaptations Provided by the Local Conferences of Bishops
A. The right to adapt the Roman ritual to the specific needs and customs of a region are noted. These adaptations must be reviewed by the Apostolic See before implementation.

Key Quote
Father, by your plan man and woman are united, and married life has been established as the one blessing that was not forfeited by original sin or washed away in the flood. Look with love upon this woman, your daughter, now joined to her husband in marriage. She asks your blessing. Give her the grace of love and peace. May she always follow the example of the holy women whose praises are sung in the Scriptures.

May her husband put his trust in her and recognize that she is his equal and the heir with him to the life of grace. May he always honor her and love her as Christ loves his bride, the Church. (Nuptial Blessing "A")

…The Church takes part in your joy and with an open heart receives you, together with your parents and friends, on the day in which before God our Father you establish between yourselves a partnership of the whole of your lives… (Unofficial translation of the second introduction to the celebration as contained in the *Revised Edition of the Marriage Liturgy*.)

Suggested Reading
National Conference of Catholic Bishops. *Revised Edition of the Marriage Liturgy* in *Bishops' Committee on the Liturgy Newsletter.* vol. XXVII, January 1991. pp. 1-4. *Ordo Celebrandi Matrimonium.* Editio Typica Altera, Vatican City: Vatican Polyglot Press, 1991.

Codex Canonum Ecclesiarum Orientalium

The Code of Canon Law of the Eastern Churches
Pope John Paul II
October 18, 1990

Major Areas of Concern
- The sacramental nature of marriage (cc. 776–782)
- Pastoral care and what must precede the celebration of marriage (cc. 783–789)
- Diriment impediments to marriage (cc. 790–812)
- Mixed marriages (cc. 813–816)
- Matrimonial consent (817–827)
- The form of the celebration of marriage (cc. 828–842)
- The convalidation of marriages (cc. 843–847)
- The separation of spouses (cc. 863–866)

The vision of the Second Vatican Council guided the formation of the revised codes of Church Law. The *Code of Canon Law for the Latin Rite* was promulgated by the Holy See in October 1983. The *Code of Canons for the Oriental Church* was promulgated in 1990.

The development of a unified code of canon law among the various churches of the Oriental rites was gradual; it occurred over a lengthy period of about one hundred fifty years. The effort was begun under Pius IX and a substantial portion of the code was promulgated by Pope Pius XII in 1945. The finished code was accepted by Pope John Paul II on October 1, 1990 and finally promulgated on October 18.

The organization of the Oriental code differs from that of the Latin. The points of law were gathered under titles, whereas the Latin arrangement gathers the codes into books. The Oriental terms (eparch, hierarch, eparchy) that correspond to those of the Latin church (bishop/ordinary, diocese) are used throughout and may confuse those unfamiliar with them.

The importance of this code cannot be overlooked, as these canons reflect the insight of the council and the rich spirituality of the Oriental churches. The pastoral and liturgical practices of these rites touch upon the lives of the faithful throughout the world. These canons are of particular importance for understanding the theology and practice of the eastern churches. In cases of inter-ritual marriage, these considerations are vital. The glossary of Latin terms and the tables of corresponding canons are most helpful for those who desire to compare the Oriental and Latin codes.

I. Chapter VII: Marriage

A. Marriage between husband and wife is a covenant and partnership.

    1. This covenant is ordered to the good of the spouses and the procreation and education of children. Through the consent of the will, man and woman enter into an irrevocable covenant. (c. 776 §1)

    2. A valid marriage between the baptized persons is sacramental by that fact of being baptized. (c. 776 §2)

    3. The essential properties of marriage are unity and indissolubility. (c. 776 §3)

    4. Equal obligations and rights exist for both spouses in those things that belong to the partnership of marriage. (c. 777)

    5. Those not prohibited by law are free to marry. (c. 778)

B. The presumption in law is for the validity of the marriage until the opposite is proven. (c. 779)

C. Both divine and canon law regulate the marriage even if only one party is Catholic. Civil authority bears its competence concerning the civil effects of marriage. (c. 780 §1)

    1. Marriage between a Catholic and a baptized non-Catholic is also regulated by the church law governing the non-Catholic party. (c. 780 §2-1°, 2°)

D. The validity of marriage between two baptized non-Catholics is judged under the law binding the parties at the time of the celebration of marriage. (c. 781,1°)

1. Any form admitted by the law governing the two parties can be recognized, provided that consent is expressed publicly and marriage is celebrated with a sacred rite if one of the parties is an Eastern rite non-Catholic. (c. 781, 2°)

E. Engagements are governed by the particular law of each Church but a promise to marry does not obligate the celebration; the reparation of damages, where warranted, arises from this promise. (c. 782 §1–2)

II. Art. I–Pastoral Care and What Must Precede the Celebration of Marriage (cc. 783–789)

A. Pastoral care and marriage preparation are the responsibility of the pastors of souls. (c. 783 §1)
   1. Suitable preaching, catechesis, and the personal preparation of the parties are necessary. (c. 783 §1, 1°, 2°)
   2. Catholic parties are exhorted to receive the Holy Eucharist in the celebration of marriage. (c. 783 §2)
   3. Pastoral assistance should be provided to assist the couple in conjugal sanctity. (c. 783 §3)

B. Each particular church, after consultation with the eparchs of overlapping areas, is to issue norms that provide for the valid celebration of marriage. (c. 784)
   1. Pastors are obligated to prevent the celebration of invalid or illicit marriage. (c. 785 §1)
      a. In danger of death the spouses' testimony regarding baptism and freedom to marry is sufficient. (c. 785 §2)
   2. The Christian faithful are obligated to reveal any impediments either to the pastor or local hierarch. (c. 786)
   3. The pastor conducting the investigation of the parties must notify the pastor blessing the marriage of his findings immediately and in writing. (c. 787)
      a. If doubts remain as to the freedom to marry, the pastor must defer the matter to the local hierarch. (c. 788)
   4. The conditions where the permission of the local hierarch to bless a marriage is necessary are listed. (c. 789, 1°–6°)

III. Art. II–Diriment Impediments in General (cc. 790–799)

A. Diriment impediments are defined. (cc. 790–791)

   1. The authority for establishing diriment impediments is noted. (c. 792–793)
   2. The authority of the local hierarch in regulating and prohibiting marriage is explained. (c. 794 §1–2)
   3. The limits of the local hierarch, the local pastor, and delegated priest in dispensing from the impediments is clarified. (c. 795–796)
   4. If the impediment is discovered after everything is prepared and the marriage cannot be delayed without the probability of serious harm, the power to dispense from impediments is held by the local hierarch. Where the case is secret, that power is held by all mentioned in 796 §2. This point applies equally to convalidation. (c. 797)
   5. The local hierarch is to be informed at once of impediments dispensed under the above conditions in the external forum and recorded in the marriage register. Secret cases are recorded in the secret archives if the forum is non-sacramental unless otherwise indicated. (c. 798–799)

IV. Art. III–Impediments Specifically (cc. 800–812)

   A. A man must have completed his sixteenth year and a woman her fourteenth year to validly marry. The particular law of any church may establish an older age for the lawful celebration of marriage. (c. 800)

   B. Impotence that is perpetual and precedes the attempt to marry renders it invalid. (c. 800 §1)
   1. Where the impediment is doubtful, marriage is not to be held up until the uncertainty is removed. (c. 800 §2)
   2. Sterility of itself never invalidates marriage. (c. 800 §3)

   C. A prior bond invalidates marriage; marriage is not to be celebrated before establishing the dissolution of that bond. (c. 802 §1–2)

   D. Marriage with the unbaptized cannot be validly celebrated; if there is doubt about the baptism, validity is presumed until the opposite is established. (c. 803 §1–3)

   E. Persons in holy orders and those bound by a public perpetual vow of chastity in a religious institute cannot marry validly. (cc. 804–805)

   F. Abduction renders marriage impossible unless clear proof of freedom is given. (c. 806)

    1. The marriage of those who cause the death of a spouse in order to marry another is invalid. (c. 807)

G. Marriage is invalid in the direct line between all ancestors and descendants up to third cousins. Where doubt exists as to a relationship through blood up to first cousins marriage is never permitted. (c. 808)

H. Affinity (in-laws) invalidates a marriage in the direct line absolutely and in the collateral line to first cousins. (c. 809)

I. The impediment of public propriety arises from an invalid marriage whose common life has been established, from cohabitation, from those marriages whose proper form is lacking, and from public concubinage. It invalidates marriages of the children of these relationships who may attempt to intermarry. (c. 810 §1–2)

J. Sponsors and the baptized and the parents of the same cannot validly marry because of the spiritual bond. Conditional baptism is another case. (c. 811 §1–2)

K. Adopted children and parents are impeded in the same manner as the natural parents. (c. 812)

V. Art. IV–Mixed Marriages (cc. 813–816)

A. The permission of the competent authority is necessary in a mixed marriage. (c. 813)

B. The local hierarch may grant the permission where

    1. the Catholic declares the willingness to remain faithful to the Church and promises to do all that is possible to have all the children baptized and educated in the Catholic Church.

    2. The other party is made aware of this promise and obligation at an appropriate time.

    3. Both parties are instructed on the nature of marriage. (c. 814)

C. The manner of these promises and the evidence of them and how the non-Catholic party is informed of this is set under the particular law of each Church. (c. 815)

D. Local hierarchs and the pastors are to support the Catholic spouse in fulfilling these obligations, and foster family unity. (816)

Art. V–Matrimonial Consent (817–827)

A. Matrimonial consent occurs in the giving and accepting of each other in order to establish marriage; no human power can replace this consent. (c. 817 §1–2)

B. Those who lack the sufficient use of reason or seriously lack judgment concerning the essentials of marriage or are incapable of assuming the essential obligations of marriage due to psychic causes cannot contract marriage. (c. 818, 1°–3°)

C. Valid consent requires at least the awareness of the essential nature and ends of marriage. (c. 819)

D. Error about the person makes a marriage invalid, but error about the quality of the person, unless it was directly intended, does not. (c. 820 §1–2)

E. Fraud that forms the grounds for consent invalidates marriage. (c. 821)

F. Error concerning the essentials of marriage makes a marriage invalid only when it determines the will to marry. (c. 822)

G. Knowledge or opinion about the nullity of a marriage may not exclude valid consent. (c. 823)

H. The presumption is for consent in agreement with the words or signs used in celebrating the sacrament, but a positive act of the will to exclude marriage, some essential element, or property of marriage invalidates the marriage. (c. 824)

I. Force or grave external fear, even if unintentional, and of the type that compels a person to choose matrimony in order to be freed from it renders that marriage invalid. (c. 825)

J. Marriages based on a condition are invalid. (c. 826)

K. Consent is presumed valid until proved otherwise. (c. 827)

VII. Art. VI–The Form of the Celebration of Marriage (cc. 828–842)

A. Valid marriages must be celebrated with a sacred rite and according to the conditions specified by law. (c. 828 §1–2)

B. Local hierarchs and pastors legitimately holding office validly bless the marriages of their subjects. (c. 829)

C. The faculty to bless a given marriage can be delegated by the local hierarch and pastor to priests of any Church, even the Latin Rite.

For validity the faculty must be expressly given to specific priests; if given in general it must be in writing. (c. 830 §1–3)

D. Local hierarchs and pastors licitly bless marriages only after their competence to do so is clearly established.

E. Marriages are celebrated before the groom's pastor unless otherwise dictated by local law or just cause. (c. 831 §1–2)

F. Marriages can be celebrated before witnesses alone under the following conditions: no priest is available without grave inconvenience, the danger of death is present; otherwise the circumstances are determined as likely to continue for a month. (c. 832 §1)
  1. If another priest, even a non-Catholic one, can be called to bless the marriage, he should be. (c. 832 §2)
  2. Where the marriage takes place before witnesses only, the spouses are to receive the blessing from the priest as soon as possible. (c. 832 §3)

G. The faculty of blessing the marriages of members of Eastern non-Catholic Churches can be given to any Catholic priest by the local hierarch under specified conditions. (c. 833 §1–2)

H. The canonical form for marriage is to be observed where one party was baptized or received into the Catholic Church; where the Catholic party is of an Eastern rite the blessing of the priest is required for validity; the form is observed for liceity. (c. 834 §1–2)

I. Dispensation from the form of marriage is reserved to the Holy See or the patriarch and is granted only for a most grave cause. (c. 835)

J. The prescriptions of the liturgical books and the legitimate customs are to be observed in the celebration of marriage. (c. 836)

K. Both parties must be present at the same time and manifest consent mutually for validity in marriage. Marriage by proxy is invalid unless particular law establishes otherwise, and is valid only where the conditions of that law are provided. (837 §1–2)

L. Marriages are to be celebrated in a parish Church or with permission in another sacred place. Marriages in other places cannot be celebrated without the permission of the local hierarch. The times and norms for marriages are established by the particular churches. (c. 838 §1–2)

M. Only one religious observance of the same marriage is permitted; celebrations in which both Catholic and non-Catholic ministers ask for the consent are forbidden. (c. 839)

N. The permission for secret marriages, the conditions under which they can take place, and the manner of recording them is described. (c. 840 §1–3)

O. Marriages are to be recorded in the marriage and baptismal registers following their celebration according to the manner prescribed by the proper eparch. The obligations of the pastor in this matter is specified. Where marriage occurs before witnesses only, they are obligated to report it to the local authority as soon as possible. (c. 841 §1–3)

P. Notation in both the marriage and baptismal records is to be made of convalidations in the external order, declarations of nullity, and legitimate dissolutions. The pastor of the place of the celebration bears this responsibility. (c. 842)

VIII. Art. VII–Convalidation of Marriage (cc. 843–847)

A. Simple Convalidation (cc. 843–857)

1. Where impeded by a diriment impediment, that obstacle must cease or be dispensed and the party aware of the impediment must renew consent. This renewal of consent is required for validity. (c. 843 §1–2)

2. The renewal of consent must be a new act of the will of the party renewing consent. (c. 844)

3. In the case of a public impediment, consent needs to be renewed by the parties according to canonical form; where occult, the consent needs to be renewed by the party who is aware of the obstacle or by both parties if both are aware of the impediment. Consent may be renewed in secret in this case. (c. 845 §1–2)

4. In the case of defective consent, validity occurs when consent is given by the party who has not consented. If this defect cannot be proven, consent may be given privately and in secret. Canonical form is required if that defect of consent can be established. (c. 846 §1–2)

5. Marriages that are invalid due to a defective form must be contracted anew according to that form to become valid. (c. 847)

B. Radical Sanation (cc. 848–852)

1. Radical sanation and its scope are defined. (c. 848–852)

2. The limits of hierarchical authority in the granting of sanations are established. Distinctions between patriarchal, eparchial, and Apostolic authority are clarified. (c. 852)

IX. Art. VIII–The Separation of Spouses (cc. 863–866)

A. Dissolution of the Bond (cc. 853–862)

1. The sacramental bond of marriage for a consummated marriage is dissolved only by death. (c. 853)

2. The dissolution of non-sacramental marriages by means of the Pauline privilege is explained. (c. 854 §1–2)

3. The conditions for the possibility for remarriage of the baptized party are specified. (c. 855 §1–2)

4. The procedures for the interrogation of the parties in the Pauline privilege are defined. (c. 856 §1– 3)

5. The right of the baptized party to celebrate a new marriage with a Catholic party is established and the conditions for it are specified. (c. 857)

6. Marriage with non-Catholics under the Pauline privilege lies under the direction of the local hierarch. (c. 858)

7. The question of regularizing polygamous marriages is addressed and norms set out. (c. 859)

8. The restoration of cohabitation in cases of Pauline privilege is prohibited. (c. 860)

9. In doubtful cases, the favor of law is given to the faith. (c. 861)

10. The dissolution of non-consummated marriages lies in the competence of the Roman Pontiff. (c. 862)

B. Separation While the Bond Continues (863–866)

1. Recommendations and conditions concerning the ending of conjugal living are made clear. Adultery is referred to explicitly. (c. 863)

2. Legitimate reasons and procedures for separation other than in the case of adultery are listed. Provisions for the well being of children and the resumption of conjugal life are made clear. (cc. 864–966)

Key Quotes

Matrimonial consent is an act of the will by which a man and woman, through an irrevocable covenant, mutually give and accept each other in order to establish marriage. (c. 817 §1)

No human power can replace this matrimonial consent. (c. 817 §2)

Only those marriages are valid which are celebrated with a sacred rite, in the presence of the local hierarch, local pastor, or a priest who has been given the faculty of blessing the marriage by either of them, and at least two witnesses, according, however to the prescriptions of the following canons, with due regard for the exceptions mentioned in canons 832 and 834 §2. (c. 828 §1)

That rite which is considered a sacred rite is the intervention of a priest assisting and blessing. (c. 828 §2)

Although it is earnestly recommended that a spouse, moved by charity and concern for the good of the family, not refuse pardon to an adulterous partner and not break up conjugal life, nevertheless, if the spouse has not expressly or tacitly condoned the misdeed of the other spouse, the former does have the right to end conjugal living, unless he or she consented to the adultery, gave cause for it, or likewise committed adultery. (c. 863 §1)

Suggested Readings

Code of Canon Law: Latin-English Edition. Washington, D.C.: Canon Law Society of America, 1983.

Code of Canons of the Eastern Church: Latin-English Edition. Washington, D.C.: Canon Law Society of America, 1990.

Schillebeeckx, Edward, O.P. *Marriage: Human Reality and Saving Mystery*. London: Sheed and Ward, 1965.

The Contribution of Pope John Paul II

The contribution of the popes within the field of marriage and family is strongly evident in the papal teachings of the past century. It is nowhere more clearly seen than within the writings and exhortations of Pope John Paul II. The present pontiff's contribution represents an integration of the prior teachings within a personalist framework. At present, his body of writings is the most extensive of any twentieth-century pope.

Karol Wojtyla was born in 1920 in Wadowice, Poland. His parents, brother, and sister died during his youth. The extent to which this tempers his appreciation of family issues is a matter of speculation. Before the Nazi occupation of Poland, Wojtyla studied at the Jagiellonian University. When the Nazis closed the university, Karol found a clandestine theater group an outlet for his artistic expressions. During the Nazi occupation, Wojtyla began to study for the priesthood and was ordained by Archbishop Sapieha in 1946. Following his ordination, Wojtyla studied mystical theology under the French theologian Fr. Reginald Garrigou-Lagrange, O.P. Garrigou-Lagrange's emphasis on the individual as the ground for theological reflection resulted in the clear direction of Wojtyla's thinking.

Completing a doctorate in theology in Rome, Wojtyla returned to Poland to complete a second doctorate in philosophy. His philosophical education drew him into the school of phenomenological realism. The impact of this school of thought is summarized by Fr. Richard Hogan in the volume *Covenant of Love* :

He saw that phenomenology was not only an excellent tool for presenting his central insight about men and women, but that it was also most practical because it was most effective. Karol Wojtyla realized that in some way phenomenology captures the attention of the twentieth century...with a conviction and force that even the system of Saint Thomas cannot approach. (Hogan, 4)

John Paul II's works include his doctoral dissertations on John of the Cross and on Husserl. Both illustrate his grasp of the philosophical and theological scope of a phenomenological method. Other works include *Sign of Contradiction, Love and Responsibility, The Acting Person*, and *Sources of Renewal: The Implementation of Vatican II.*

Karol Wojtyla, an enthusiastic parish priest, seminary professor, spiritual director, and writer was ordained auxiliary bishop of Krakow in 1958. In 1964 he became the Archbishop of Krakow and was named a cardinal three years later. Throughout, he continued a schedule of teaching and writing. He continues to refine the teachings of his predecessors using this phenomenological method.

His first encyclical, *Redemptor Hominis*, serves as the basis for his subsequent teaching. John Paul II is clear in his affirmation of the necessity of the human person in relationship.

Man cannot live without love. He remains a being that is incomprehensible for himself, his life is senseless, if love is not revealed to him, if he does not encounter love, if he does not experience it and make it his own, if he does not participate intimately in it. (¶25)

He further states:

The Church's fundamental function in every age and particularly in ours is to direct man's gaze, to point the awareness and experience of the whole of humanity towards the mystery of God, to help all men to be familiar with the profundity of the Redemption taking place in Christ Jesus. (¶27)

John Paul II developed his teachings on marriage and the family through the Apostolic Exhortation *Familiaris Consortio* (1981) and through the Wednesday Catechesis, a series of sixty-three papal addresses beginning in September 1979 and concluding in May 1981. An

English translation of this catechesis is available in two related works: *Original Unity of Man and Woman* and *Blessed are the Pure of Heart*. From July to November 1984, John Paul II led the faithful through a reflection on Paul VI's encyclical *Humanae Vitae*. This concluded a four-year instruction concerning the sacramentality and redemption of the body.

The themes of human love and dignity, the necessity of interpersonal relationship, the critical role of marriage and family life appear throughout his encyclicals and world-wide addresses to the faithful. It is inadvisable to separate the social teachings of John Paul II because of his estimation of the divine plan unfolding within the sacrament of marriage and within the human family. The connection made between the dignity of human labor and the family in *Laborem Exercens* illustrates this coherence:

> ... the family constitutes one of the most important terms of reference for shaping the social and ethical order of human work...In fact, the family is simultaneously a community made possible by work and the first school of work, within the home, for every person. (¶43)

The establishment of the Pontifical Council on the Family and the Pontifical John Paul II Institute for Studies on Marriage and Family illustrate his commitment to continuing the development of Church teaching on these themes.

Catholic Social Teaching on Marriage and the Family

Over the last one hundred years the social teaching of the church on a global and local level has acknowledged issues affecting the family. Each generation has seen the church specifically address topics on the economic and social order. At the heart of these teachings is the dignity of the person in community. The most fundamental community, the family, is affected by the issues of the moment. In the earliest contemporary social teaching, Pope Leo XIII's *Rerum Novarum* focused on the workers' rights to a just wage to support themselves and their families. Pope John Paul II's one-hundred-year retrospective, *Centesimus Annus*, reaffirms this same teaching. This can also be seen in the American bishops' pastoral statement *Economic Justice for All* (1986), where they note:

> Economic life has a profound effect on all social structures and particularly on the family. A breakdown of family life often brings with it hardship and poverty. Divorce, failure to provide support to mothers and children, abandonment of children, pregnancies out of wedlock, all contribute to the amount of poverty among us. Though these breakdowns of marriage and the family are more visible among the poor, they do not affect only that one segment of our society.... (¶344)

> ...With good reason, the Church has traditionally held that the

family is the basic building-block of any society. In fighting against economic arrangements that weaken the family, the Church contributes to the well being of society...economic arrangements must support the family and support its solidarity. (¶346)

Although the following listing of specific references to marriage and families is valuable, these references need to be seen in the broader context of the documents and their historical settings.

I. **Rerum Novarum** (*The Condition of Labor*), **Encyclical Letter of Leo XIII, 1891.**
  A. Families have rights within the state, and the father, as head of the household, needs to be able to provide for his family.

  B. The state should support these rights. (¶10)

II. **Quadragesimo Anno** (*The Reconstruction of the Social Order*), **Encyclical Letter of Pope Pius XI, 1931.**
  A. Women and children should not be abused in the work world. (¶71)

III. **Pacem in Terris** (*Peace on Earth*), **Encyclical Letter of Pope John XXIII, 1963.**
  A. Everyone has a right to choose one's state in life, including rights to establish a family and pursue a religious vocation. (¶15–16)

  B. Women are participating in public life. (¶41)

IV. **Justice in the World, Statement of the Synod of Bishops, 1971.**
  A. The family is the principal agent for the education (to justice), which is a continuing process. (¶54)

V. **Evangelii Nuntiandi** (*Evangelization in the Modern World*), **Apostolic Exhortation of Pope Paul VI, 1975.**
  A. Bishops, priests, religious, laity, young people, and families all have important roles to play in evangelization. (¶68–72)

VI. **Laborem Exercens** (*On Human Work*), **Encyclical Letter of Pope John Paul II, 1981.**
  A. Work and Family Life
    1. Work makes family life possible.

2. Work makes possible the achievement of the purposes of the family.

3. Work increases the common good of the family. (¶10)

B. The Church calls for:

1. Wages sufficient to support a family;

2. Allowances to mothers raising a family;

3. Reevaluation of the mother's role to ensure the proper love for children and fair opportunities for women. (¶19)

VII. **Centesimus Annus** (*One Hundred Years*), **Encyclical Letter of Pope John Paul II, 1991.**

A. The family, founded on marriage, is the sanctuary of life. (¶39)

B. Democratic systems need to solidify their foundations by explicitly recognizing certain rights, especially the rights to life, to work, and to establish a family. (¶47)

Suggested Readings

Charles, Rodger, S.J. *The Social Teaching of Vatican II.* San Francisco: Ignatius Press, 1982.

Henriot, Peter, DeBerri, Edward P., and Schultheis, Michael J. *Catholic Social Teaching—Our Best Kept Secret* (Centenary ed.). Maryknoll, NY: Orbis Books, 1992. (3rd rev. ed.)

Shuck, Michael. *That They Be One: The Social Teaching of the Papal Encyclicals, 1740-1989.* Washington, D.C.: Georgetown University Press, 1991.

Walsh, Michael, and Davies, Brian (eds.). *Proclaiming Justice and Peace: Papal Documents from Rerum Novarum through Centesimus Annus (Revised and Expanded).* Mystic, CT: Twenty-Third Publications, 1991.

Study Questions

GENERAL QUESTIONS

1. What motivates you to study the official church teachings on marriage and family issues?

2. What is your understanding of the Catholic Church's teachings on marriage and family life?

3. Does your life experience confirm the Church's teaching? Are there experiences you have had that lead you to be challenged by the teachings of the Church?

4. What are ways that conflicts can be resolved between the teachings of the Church on specific issues and an individual's experience? What ways are helpful?

5. How do the Church's documents speak to people in the world today?

6. Do the themes gathered in this text (pages 12-14) emerge within homilies, adult education classes, or the general reading you have encountered? Are any of these themes new to you?

7. How would you go about presenting these issues to others?

8. Which topics emerge as controversial within the discussion of friends and family members? Why?

9. As you review these documents, can you notice any move forward in the emphasis of the teachings of the Church?

10. Are there common themes emerging from these documents? How are they connected? Is there coherence among them?

11. How are the "ends" of marriage presented in Church documents?

12. How has the understanding of marriage as a contract and covenant changed within these documents? Can you locate specific documents that illustrate this change?

13. Over the past one hundred years, how has the structure of the family changed?

14. Why did the Church address these changes within formal documents rather than through less formal methods?

15. Some may say there is no real need for the *average Catholic* to have a knowledge of these documents. How much of these teachings should be known by the faithful? Should the clergy and religious have a better knowledge of these materials than the average Catholic?

ARCANUM

1. How did the social situation of the nineteenth century lead to economic and cultural changes?

2. Pope Leo XIII guided the Catholic Church from 1878 until 1903. How does his encyclical *Arcanum* (*On Christian Marriage*) address the tension between Church and state regarding marriage and the formation of family life?

3. How does Leo XIII speak to marriage and family life as a Christian vocation? Explain.

CODE OF CANON LAW, 1917

1. Compare and contrast the canonical definitions of marriage found within the 1917 code and the 1983 code. See key quotes on pp. 20 and 70.

2. Do any features within the documents written between these two periods point to a change in emphasis?

3. The 1917 code mentions the "ends" of marriage. How do these concepts express the reality of conjugal life?

CASTI CONNUBII

1. What social issues are addressed in this document?

2. Do they differ significantly from present-day concerns? How would you account for this?

3. What is the role of children in marriage?

4. How is the issue of responsible parenting and family planning treated?

5. How does this encyclical present marriage as the foundation for authentic family life?

6. Contrast the major concerns of this document with those of *Arcanum*.

VEGLIARE CON SOLLECITUDINE
1. How does this document differ from the others presented in this book?

2. What is the significance of this statement?

3. How did the changes in medical technology touch upon the family issues of the day?

4. Pius XII encouraged professional competence of midwives in their care of married couples. What specific ways can midwives assist couples in their vocation?

5. In this document, how does Pius XII view sexuality in marriage?

6. How is the issue of family planning presented? Discuss.

NELL'ORDINE DELLA
1. In this document, what does Pius XII say about the dignity of human life from the moment of conception?

2. What are the major areas of concern raised here?

3. How does this address relate to *Familiaris Consortio* and the *Charter of the Rights of the Family*?

4. How does Pius XII advocate for family life in this address?

VATICAN II
1. How does the treatment of the purposes of marriage compare with prior documents, especially the code of 1917?

2. What are the points of unity and difference in the approach taken in the Vatican II era regarding the conjugal bond of love? How do they differ from that of the Vatican I era?

3. Discuss the key quote from *Lumen Gentium* (p. 41).

MIXED MARRIAGES

1. How do Protestant, Orthodox, and Roman Catholic Christians differ in their understanding of sacramental marriage?

2. What is the present attitude of the Roman Catholic Church toward the marriages of Protestants and Orthodox Christians? Is this attitude observed in documents written prior to Vatican II?

3. What elements are most significant in these two documents?

4. How do these documents address the question of the religious formation of children within these unions?

HUMANAE VITAE

1. The responsibility of family life emerges from the bond between the spouses. How does *Humanae Vitae* present this teaching?

2. Is this a departure from, or affirmation of, prior papal statements?

3. What philosophical/theological framework does this document emerge from?

4. What specific methods of birth regulation are morally acceptable? Explain the reasoning.

5. How can the Church's teaching in the area of family planning support married life and family development?

6. Compare the key quotes of *Humanae Vitae* with that of *Vegliare Con Sollecitudine*.

7. How does the teaching of *Humanae Vitae* on this matter compare with that of *Casti Connubii*?

HUMAN LIFE IN OUR DAY

1. What was the purpose of this document?

2. What was the significance of the discussion of the role of conscience in this document?

3. How is theological dissent presented in this document?

PERSONA HUMANA

1. What specific issues does this document address? What methodology is put forth in responding to the concerns?

2. Where do we find the fundamental principles of life? Are these changeable?

3. In moral matters is the individual the sole judge of his destiny? What is the Catholic view of this question?

4. How has the Church viewed this question since Vatican II? What is the ground for, and are there limits to, dissent in sexual moral matters?

FAMILIARIS CONSORTIO
1. Identify the four purposes of the family.

2. How can these purposes advance the human situation in the modern world?

3. What rights need to be promoted among governments to advance human dignity?

4. How does the vision of human freedom affect the understanding of family life?

5. In what ways does this exhortation present the Church's pastoral concern for the well being of the family?

THE CODE OF CANON LAW, 1983
1. Compare and contrast the key quotes from the 1917 and 1983 codes. How and why are they different? In what ways are they similar?

2. How does the advance of the social sciences impact upon the concepts of marriage as seen in this code?

3. How do these affect the concept of matrimonial consent?

4. How does the 1983 code address the issue of the "ends" of marriage?

CHARTER OF RIGHTS OF THE FAMILY
1. What specific rights of the family are neglected in the modern world? What tangible proposal does this document make in responding to this?

2. Are any previous papal documents forerunners of these propositions?

PASTORAL CARE OF THE HOMOSEXUAL

1. What are the pastoral recommendations made to provide care for the homosexual person?

2. Is this concern reflected in any prior documentation?

3. What is the church's clear teaching and pastoral response in this area?

4. How does this document support the human dignity of the homosexual person?

5. How does this document reflect contemporary concerns in this area?

DONUM VITAE

1. Has the framework for the Church's response to medical technology changed? Compare this to Pius XII's *Vegliare Con Sollecitudine*.

2. What is the fundamental criteria for responding to this issue?

3. Does the church view the questions of artificial contraception and artificial procreation differently?

4. What pastoral concerns need to be raised when working with infertile couples?

5. At what stage of marriage preparation should this issue be approached?

MULIERIS DIGNITATEM

1. How is the dignity of women reaffirmed in Scripture?

2. How do the Gospels portray the relationship of Jesus with women? How do the statements of Jesus about marriage promote the dignity of women?

3. Contrast the conventional wisdom about gender issues with the vision of male and female in this document.

4. Are there unresolved questions regarding gender and personhood that have yet to be adequately addressed?

CHRISTIFIDELIS LAICI

1. Discuss the key quote of the document in the light of the *Charter of the Rights of the Family* and *Familiaris Consortio*.

ORDO CELEBRANDI MATRIMONIUM

1. How do the norms and guidelines listed here reflect the concerns of prior documents?

2. How is the liturgical celebration of marriage expressive of the faith of the couple?

3. What recommendations about the revised rite reflect pastoral concerns about engaged couples?

4. Discuss the key quote. How are the vision of marriage and the roles of the spouses presented?

CODEX CANONUM ECCLESIARUM ORIENTALIUM

1. How do the definitions of marriage compare between the Oriental and Latin rite codes of Law? What significance do these differences indicate?

2. How does the Oriental code address the issue of the separation of spouses? Does the Latin code address this issue in a similar manner?

3. How does the role of the priest in the Oriental code differ from that of the Latin code? How is this role the same? What does this indicate?

Bibliography

Primary Sources for Documents

For papal and Vatican documents, the official versions can be found in *Acta Apostolica Sedes.*

For English translations of the papal encyclicals, see Claudia Carlen, IHM's work listed below. It is also an excellent source of annotated bibliographies relating to each document cited.

A compilation of the Decrees of the ecumenical councils is presented in Tanner, Norman, P., S.J., ed. *Decrees of the Ecumenical Councils, Vol. 2: Trent to Vatican II,* Washington, D.C., Georgetown University Press, 1990.

The United States Catholic Conference (USCC) makes available all authoritative statements of the National Conference of Catholic Bishops as well as papal and curial documents. See their publication catalogue for any specific documents.

The Daughters of St. Paul (Boston) have compiled all of Pope John Paul II's papal writings in booklet and pamphlet forms. The papal encyclicals of the past one hundred years and Vatican statements are also available through them.

A General Bibliography

A Positive Vision for Family Life—A Resource Guide for Pope John Paul II's Apostolic Exhortation Familiaris Consortio. Rev. Thomas Lynch and Valerie Dillon, eds. Commission on Marriage and Family Life. Department of Education, USCC, 1985.

Abbott, Walter M., S.J., ed. *The Documents of Vatican II*, New York: America Press, 1966.

Albacete, Lorenzo M. *Commentary on Instruction on Respect for Human Life in its Origin and on the Dignity of Procreation*, Boston: St. Paul Editions, 1987.

Arcanum, S. Kardos in *The New Catholic Encyclopedia*, vol. 1, p. 742.

Bouscaren, T. Lincoln and Ellis, Adam C. *Canon Law: A Text and Commentary*. Milwaukee: The Bruce Publishing Company, 1957 (3rd ed.).

Carlen, Claudia, I.H.M. *Papal Pronouncements* (vols. 1-2). Raleigh, NC: The Pieran Press, 1990.

Carlen, Claudia, I.H.M. *The Papal Encyclicals* (vols. 1-5). Raleigh, NC: The Pieran Press, 1990.

Charles, Rodger, S.J. *The Social Teaching of Vatican II*. San Francisco: Ignatius Press, 1982.

Casti Connubii. S. Kardos in *The New Catholic Encyclopedia*, vol. 3, p. 190.

Code of Canon Law: Latin-English Edition. Washington, D.C.: Canon Law Society of America, 1983.

Code of Canons of the Eastern Church: Latin-English Edition. Washington, D.C.: Canon Law Society of America, 1990.

Commentary on the Documents of Vatican II. vol. I-V New York: Herder and Herder, 1969. [An extensive historical review of each document with a commentary.]

Coriden, James A. *An Introduction to Canon Law*. Mahwah, NJ: Paulist Press, 1991.

Coriden, James A., et al. *The Code of Canon Law: A Text and Commentary*. Mahwah, NJ: Paulist Press, 1985.

Doohan, Leonard. *John Paul II and the Laity*. Le Jacq Publishing, Inc., 1984.

Elliot, Peter J. *What God Has Joined: The Sacramentality of Marriage*. New York: Alba House, 1990.

Flannery, Austin, O.P., gen. ed. *The Conciliar and Post Conciliar Documents*. Northport, NY: Costello Publishing Co., 1981 ed.

Flannery, Austin, O.P., gen. ed. *Vatican Council II: More Post Conciliar*

Documents. Northport, NY: Costello Publishing Co., 1982 ed.

Ford, John C., S.J., et al. *The Teaching of Humanae Vitae: A Defense.* San Francisco: Ignatius Press, 1988.

Häring, Bernard, C.Ss.R. *The Law of Christ.* (3 vols.) Westminster, MD: Newman, 1963.

Harvey, John, O.S.F.S. *The Homosexual Person: New Thinking in Pastoral Care.* San Francisco: Ignatius Press, 1987.

Henriot, Peter, DeBerri, Edward P., and Schultheis, Michael J. *Catholic Social Teaching: Our Best Kept Secret* (Centenary Edition). Maryknoll, NY: Orbis Books, 1992. (3rd rev. ed.)

Hogan, Richard M., and LeVoir, John M. *Covenant of Love: Pope John Paul II on Sexuality, Marriage, and Family in the Modern World.* (reprint) San Francisco: Ignatius Press, 1986.

Human Life in Our Day, in *Pastoral Letters of the U.S. Bishops* (vol. 3), 1962-1974, Hugh J. Nolan, ed. Washington, D.C.: Publications Office, NCCB/USCC, 1983. pp. 164-183.

Kasper, Walter. *Theology of Christian Marriage.* New York: Crossroad Publishing, 1984.

Keane, Philip E., S.S. *Sexual Morality: A Catholic Perspective.* Paramus, NJ: Paulist Press, 1977.

Lawler, Michael. *Ecumenical Marriage and Remarriage: Gifts and Challenges to the Churches.* Mystic, CT: Twenty-Third Publications, 1990.

Lawler, Ronald, et al. *Catholic Sexual Ethics: A Summary, Explanation and Defense.* Huntington, IN: Our Sunday Visitor, 1985.

Liebard, Odile M. *Official Catholic Teachings: Love and Sexuality.* Wilmington, NC: Consortium Books, 1978.

Mackin, Theodore, S.J. *The Marital Sacrament.* New York: Paulist Press, 1989.

Mackin, Theodore, S.J. *What Is Marriage?* New York: Paulist Press, 1982.

Mathis, M., and Bonner, D. *The Pastoral Companion: A Handbook of Canon Law.* (14th ed.) Chicago: Franciscan Herald Press, 1976.

May, William E. *Sex, Marriage and Chastity: Reflections of a Catholic Layman, Spouse and Parent.* Chicago: Franciscan Herald Press, 1981.

May, William E. "The Vatican Declaration on Sexual Ethics and the Moral Methodology of Vatican II." *Linacre Quarterly*. May 1985, pp. 116-129.

McCarthy, Donald G., and Bayer, Edward J. *Handbook On Critical Sexual Issues*. Garden City, NY: Doubleday and Co. Image Books, 1984.

Morneau, Bishop Robert F. *Themes and Thesis of Six Recent Papal Documents: A Commentary*. Staten Island, NY: Alba House, 1985.

Morrisey, Francis G. *The Canonical Significance of Papal and Curial Pronouncements*. Washington, D.C.: Canon Law Society of America, 1981.

Mulligan, James J. *Choose Life*. Braintree, MA: The Pope John Center, 1991.

Mulligan, James J. *The Pope and The Theologians: The Humanae Vitae Controversy*. Mount St. Mary's Seminary Press, Emmitsburg, MD, 1968.

Paul VI. *Address to Teams of Our Lady* (May 4, 1970) in Liebard, Odile M. *Official Catholic Teachings: Love and Sexuality*, Wilmington, NC: Consortium Books, 1978, pp. 378-388.

Pius XII. *Address to Midwives* (October 29, 1951), pp. 101-122 and *Address to Associations of Larger Families* (November 26, 1951), pp. 123-127 in Liebard, Odile M. *Official Catholic Teachings: Love and Sexuality*. Wilmington, NC: Consortium Books, 1978.

Prieur, Michael R. *Married in the Lord* (rev.). Collegeville, MN: The Liturgical Press, 1978.

Saxton, Stanley L., et. al. *The Changing Family: Views from Theology and the Social Sciences in the Light of the Apostolic Exhortation Familiaris Consortio*. Chicago: Loyola University Press, 1984.

Schillebeeckx, Edward, O.P. *Marriage: Human Reality and Saving Mystery*. London: Sheed and Ward, 1965.

Shannon, Thomas A., and Cahill, Lisa Sowle. *Religion and Artificial Reproduction: An Inquiry into the Vatican "Instruction on Respect for Human Life in Its Origin and on the Dignity of the Human Person."* New York: Crossroad Publishing, 1988.

Shuck, Michael. *That They Be One: The Social Teaching of the Papal Ency-clicals, 1740-1989.* Washington, D.C.: Georgetown University Press, 1991.

Smith, Janet E. *Humanae Vitae: A Generation Later.* Washington, D.C.: The Catholic University of America Press, 1991.

Tanner, Norman P., S.J. *Decrees of the Ecumenical Councils,* vols. 1–2. Washington, D.C.: Georgetown University Press, 1990.

The Family Center for Love and Life. Boston: Daughters of St. Paul Press.

Thomas, J. L., S.J. *The Catholic Viewpoint On Marriage and the Family.* Garden City: Doubleday, 1958.

USCC. *Human Sexuality: A Catholic Perspective for Education and Lifelong Learning.* Washington, D.C.: USCC Publications Office, 1991.

Von Hildebrand, Dietriech. *The Encyclical Humanae Vitae: A Sign of Con-tradiction.* Chicago: Franciscan Herald Press, 1969.

Walsh, Michael, and Davies, Brian (eds.). *Proclaiming Justice and Peace: Documents from John XXIII to John Paul II.* Mystic, CT: Twenty-Third Publications, 1991.

Williams, Bruce, O.P. "Homosexuality: The New Vatican Statement," in *Theological Studies 48* (1987), 259-277.

Wojtyla, K. (John Paul II). *Frutiful and Responsible Love.* New York: Sea-bury Press, 1979.

Wojtyla, K. (John Paul II). *Love and Responsibility.* New York: Farrar, Straus, Giroux, 1981.

Wojtyla, K. (John Paul II). *Reflections on Humanae Vitae: Conjugal Morali-ty.* Boston: St. Paul Editions, 1984.

Wrenn, Lawrence. *Annulments.* (4th ed. rev.) Washington, D.C.: Canon Law Society of America, 1983.

Of Related Interest...

Dynamics of Marriage
Love, Sex and Growth from a Christian Perspective
Jack Dominian

A noted psychiatrist and marriage counselor looks at how married couples can approach their problems, concerns and lifestyles in a way that is both Christian and contemporary. ISBN: 0-89622-563-1, 176 pp, $9.95

A Decision to Love
A Marriage Preparation Program
John M.V. Midgley and Susan Vollmer Midgley

This program is based on the realization that in a world of complex relationships, couples need to love with their heads as well as with their hearts. Exercises and questions help couples explore their feelings. (Leader's guide also available.) ISBN: 0-89622-514-3, 128 pp, $6.50

Ecumenical Marriage and Remarriage
Gifts and Challenges to the Churches
Michael Lawler

The author challenges churches to recognize the gift of grace inherent in couples involved in ecumenical marriages and in remarriages.
ISBN: 0-89622-441-4, 112 pp, $8.95

Making Your Marriage Work
Growing in Love After Falling in Love
Christopher C. Reilly

This book looks at marriage from a positive, growth-oriented perspective, emphasizing communication, accommodation and acceptance as cornerstones for building a strong marital bond. ISBN: 0-89622-387-6, 164 pp, $7.95

Secular Marriage, Christian Sacrament
Michael Lawler

This book seeks to uncover the very essence of Christian marriage, an essence that resides in the faith of the baptized, believing couple. It examines the distinction between secular marriage and Christian sacrament, recognizing that each exists in response to specific needs. ISBN: 0-89622-273-x, 140 pp, $8.95

Available at religious bookstores or from

TWENTY-THIRD PUBLICATIONS
P.O. Box 180 • Mystic, CT 06355
1-800-321-0411